Discipling in the Church

Recovering a Ministry of the Gospel

Marlin Jeschke

Foreword by James M. Lapp

Herald Press
Scottdale, Pennsylvania
Kitchener, Ontario

Library of Congress Cataloging-in-Publication Data

Jeschke, Marlin.
  Discipling in the church : recovering a ministry of the gospel /
Marlin Jeschke ; foreword by James M. Lapp. — 3rd ed., rev. and
enl.
      p.   cm.
  Rev. ed. of: Discipling the brother. 1972.
  Bibliography: p.
  Includes indexes.
  ISBN 0-8361-3480-X (pbk. : alk. paper)
  1. Church discipline.   I. Jeschke, Marlin. Discipling the
brother.   II. Title.
BV740.J47 1988   88-21475
262.9—dc19   CIP

The paper used in this publication meets the minimum requirements of
American National Standard for Information Sciences—Permanence of
Paper for Printed Library Materials, ANSI Z39.48-1984.

About the cover: The cover graphic shows the clasped hands of two persons
walking side-by-side. The graphic was chosen to symbolize the mutuality and
caring of the discipling process. Photograph by Robert L. Blosser.

Unless otherwise specified, Scripture references are from the Revised Standard Version of the Bible, copyrighted 1946, 1952, © 1971, 1973.

DISCIPLING IN THE CHURCH
Copyright © 1972, 1979, 1988 by Herald Press, Scottdale, Pa. 15683. Third
edition, revised and enlarged. Earlier editions entitled *Discipling the Brother.*
    Published simultaneously in Canada by Herald Press,
    Kitchener, Ont. N2G 4M5. All rights reserved.
Library of Congress Catalog Card Number: 88-21475
International Standard Book Number: 0-8361-3480-X
Printed in the United States of America
Design by Gwen M. Stamm

1   2   3   4   5   6   7   8   95   94   93   92   91   90   89   88

Discipling
in the
Church

If your brother sins against you,
go and tell him his fault,
between you and him alone.
If he listens to you,
you have gained your brother.
But if he does not listen,
take one or two others along with you,
that every word may be confirmed by the evidence of two or
three witnesses.
If he refuses to listen to them,
tell it to the church;
And if he refuses to listen even to the church,
let him be to you as a Gentile and a tax collector.

Truly, I say to you,
whatever you bind on earth shall be bound in heaven,
and whatever you loose on earth shall be loosed in heaven.
—*Matthew 18:15-18*

Gratis

99338

CONTENTS

PART TWO

FOREWORD

Currently, church growth and evangelism are recovering a rightful centrality in many segments of the church. The question may appropriately be asked, "What will be the character of the new congregations that are planted?" *Discipling in the Church* helpfully contributes solid teaching on what it means to develop bodies of believers that are true alternatives to a bland, generic Christianity.

In this volume Marlin Jeschke provides a fresh and thorough look at Matthew 18:15-20 and other New Testament passages pertinent to discipline. For those pastors and congregations serious about resisting narcissism and enabling a spiritually interdependent community of God's people to emerge, this book offers foundational insights. Professor Jeschke gently but firmly calls us to the relevance of Christ's way for the community of believers as we move toward the twenty-first century.

The language of discipline is finding new acceptance in the church. Admittedly, the reception is still mixed. But in many congregations there is evident discontent with innocuous definitions of membership. The notion of accountability now commonly accepted in business relationships is again being viewed as a necessary component in the body life of the local church.

To be sure, discipline is only one dimension of responsible church membership. Mutual care of one another, affirmation of spiritual gifts, distribution of material resources to those in need, and discernment on issues of ethical concern are all necessary aspects of authentic life in Christ's body. But when congregations neglect discipline, the character of an otherwise warm fellowship can grow soft and ineffectual. Authentic community calls for attention to both interpersonal support (inclusion) and clarity about boundaries for the members (which may involve exclusion). Generally we do better in being supportive than we do in being confrontive in church relationships.

Social scientists are now joining with Christian leaders in identifying the insidiousness of individualism in North American society. God's people are not immune to these forces. The counsel to do what feels good and look out for yourself is heard on every quarter. Is it possible to experience genuine *koinonia* in the last years of the twentieth century? This book suggests it is if members exercise healthy loving regard for one another in both supportive and corrective ways.

The natural reflex to the word *discipline* continues to be negative for a great many people. There can be no defense for seeming harsh or capricious behavior by church leaders of the past. In reaction to such severity an era of permissiveness predominated in many congregations. Thankfully, there are small signs that renewed emphasis on discipline and mutual accountability is welcomed in many churches, especially among newer and younger members.

I am honored and delighted to commend this book to all readers who are on the quest toward the high calling of discipleship within the context of Christian community. Small groups, Sunday school classes, elders, and pastors all will profit from its study. Allow its message to prod and probe, convict and correct, until we all become "mature in Christ."

—*James M. Lapp*
Executive Secretary
Mennonite Church General Board
May 13, 1988

ACKNOWLEDGMENTS

I owe thanks to two people for their contribution to my study of the subject of this book. They are John W. Miller, who first suggested I write my doctoral dissertation on this topic, and Professor William Hordern, my adviser in the doctoral program. Indeed, I also owe them an apology for not acknowledging them in earlier editions.

My wife Charmaine typed the draft for the first edition of this book in 1972 and has generously given her editorial skills through several drafts of this edition. I am also indebted to Lois Barrett and Al Meyer for helpful suggestions.

Thanks are due to Marta Brunner, my student assistant, who put much of this manuscript onto disks, and to Loren Johns, theology book editor of Herald Press, who proposed a revised third edition and has seen this manuscript through publication.

Thanks, finally, to the many people—more than I could recall here—who have participated in many seminars in many churches over many years. In this way they have contibuted to my—and the church's—continuing work with this important subject.

INTRODUCTION

Mention church discipline, and it conjures up mixed feelings in today's average church members. On the one hand, they intuitively recognize some need for it. After all, the Bible teaches it, and without church discipline the significance of church membership is soon undercut. On the other hand, they have bad memories of unloving acts of church discipline in the past. Sometimes church leaders have acted in authoritarian, legalistic ways on issues that have had little connection with spiritual life.

Too often, unfortunately, it is the bad feelings that persist in the average church members' minds. So if someone suggests a recovery of church discipline today, their conditioned reflex is, "No thanks." They are grateful that witch-hunting, the Inquisition, and similar ecclesiastical nightmares are a thing of the past. But this attitude may be a somewhat hasty reaction. It would be too bad if we made ourselves the victims of other people's past mistakes.

> To abandon discipline because it has sometimes been ill-administered is as unwarranted as it would be to abandon wor-

ship on the ground that it has sometimes been ill-conducted.
The relaxation of discipline has often more absurd results than
ever attended its excess.[1]

Or take the example of marriage. We don't abandon the institution of marriage simply because of bad notions of marriage
or bad marriages. Rather, we try to recover good views of marriage and good marriages.

Or, as John White says, "Law is abused. Should we therefore
opt for [anarchy]?"[2] The answer to bad church discipline is
good church discipline, not no church discipline.

The problem with church discipline is partly a matter of
terminology. The term has acquired bad connotations. Unfortunately, it is not easy to find a better one. The terms *mission* and *evangelism* are still good and generally accepted positive terms. Although some people have done outrageous things
in the history of missions and evangelism, these terms are still
used positively today to identify important and indispensable
ministries of the church.

Ministry is, of course, another term that recent American
Christianity has tarnished. TV programs and businesses (even
rackets) are called "ministries." But we speak here of ministry
in the proper sense of that term: the cause of presenting the
message of Christ to liberate people from evil and to lead them
into Christ's way.

Church discipline is a ministry inseparably related to and
continuous with evangelism and missions. Evangelism and missions seek to bring people into Christ's way, the way of discipleship. Similarly, church discipline seeks to keep these people in
Christ's way or restore to that way those who for some reason
are straying or have strayed from it. The word *discipline* comes
from the same root as the word *disciple*.

Evangelism and church discipline are both acts of discipling.
There is a continuity between them. Jesus called his disciples,
instructed and corrected them, restored a Peter who had

denied him, and "excommunicated" a Judas. In the same way the church today calls people into Christ's way. It then instructs them in that way and, if necessary, corrects and restores them to the Christian way. If necessary, the church also recognizes and respects some people's abandonment of the Christian way.

This book does not discuss some practices often called discipline such as gathered worship, the study of Scripture, public and private prayer, and even fasting. These are not just good. They are indispensable in the Christian life and the life of the church. Yet in themselves they are not enough. The church can and must have recourse to corrective discipline where self-discipline breaks down. Isolating such a subject for special attention does not at all imply that we lose sight of other tasks of the church. On the contrary, it is the comprehensive view that enables us to recover a healthy practice of corrective church discipline.

We have already used the term *corrective discipline.* One could also speak of *remedial* discipline. One writer chooses the term *exceptional* discipline.

Church discipline, as we use the term in this book, refers to the ministry of discipling a Christian brother or sister whose spiritual health and life are endangered by a particular act or attitude. It is the way Christ taught "for restoring sinning saints."[3]

Writers have used many terms for the critical problem that invites discipline: *to err, sin, transgress,* or *trespass.* One can also speak of a violation of covenant, of unfaith, of a lapse, even of apostasy. It can be a matter of conduct, behavior, an act. Or it can be a spirit, an attitude, a lifestyle. It can be *backsliding,* as one old term had it. It can be a lack in attendance, interest, or association with the church through secularization, changed relationships, or geographical relocation.

Church discipline literature often speaks of an *offender,* perhaps because the classical liturgy of many church traditions spoke of "offending" God's holy laws and of being "miserable offenders." We will use the terms *offender, erring saint,* and *someone in spiritual trouble* interchangeably to speak of someone in need of special spiritual help.

I hope the reader can catch the idea of the special focus intended in this book. *Church discipline* here is analogous to crisis intervention in medicine. Certain infections, symptoms of cancer, heart disease, or injury in auto accidents all signal the need for special help. They are something more than a cold, the flu, a scratched finger, or a minor bruise. Unless help is forthcoming in emergency situations, the result is very possibly death. In the spiritual realm there are similar "red flag" signals of serious danger to spiritual health and life. There is room for a study such as the present book on this kind of emergency spiritual care.

Unfortunately, the importance, value, and genuinely evangelical rationale of church discipline are still not widely enough appreciated in today's Christianity. This is true in both so-called mainline and evangelical churches. The sparse literature on the subject attests to that.

When this book first appeared in 1972, I felt like the proverbial lonely "voice crying in the wilderness." Since then eight monographs and many magazine articles on the subject have come to my notice. I am encouraged by these additional voices joining the dialogue. I happily recognize them in the notes and bibliography. This revised edition is the better, I hope, for their contributions.

We have said enough now to explain the general subject and focus of this book and the meaning of its most basic terms. We have also shown that church discipline—like missions and evangelism—is a necessary part of the church's life. Again, like missions and evangelism, church discipline properly conducted is not harsh, vindictive, unloving, or unchristian. It is the compassionate effort to preserve people in the way of faith or to restore them to it.

This book is an attempt, then, to work toward an evangelical understanding of church discipline, that is, a church discipline according to the gospel. It is a discipline defined by the gospel and conducted according to the gospel.

This study is not primarily an examination of church discipline in the New Testament, although almost all New Testament texts addressing the subject come under discussion in what follows. Nor is this a historical study, although we frequently refer to the doctrine and practice of the church in its history in order to learn from its record. Not enough people see the value of examining the church's historical record of dealing with sin in the church. That is the point at which some writers' problem begins. They propose to formulate a doctrine and practice of church discipline from the Scriptures while unconsciously reading the Scriptures through the glasses of a particular post-biblical ecclesiastical tradition.

This book is an attempt to recover a healthy understanding and practice of church discipline by going to the classic text on the subject, Matthew 18:15-18. We shall attempt to portray systematically what discipline based on the gospel looks like from beginning to end, from recognition of a problem of sin to its resolution in forgiveness or excommunication. Such discipline, it is hoped, will result in the restoration of a Christian brother or sister. If we take for our model what Jesus taught his disciple community, we will have a sound beginning in the recovery of authentic church discipline and healthy church life today.

Matthew 18 says, "If your *brother* sins." The gender in this text may be a problem for some people. It is doubtful that Jesus specifically intended to exclude the sisters by this statement. Whatever the original intent, both brothers and sisters may stand in need of help. Both sisters and brothers have the privilege and responsibility of giving help. The whole family of God is in this ministry together.

This book has two parts. The seven chapters of part one contain the basic presentation of the ministry of church discipline. They offer guidance on how to reach out with help to those in spiritual trouble in order to restore them to the way of discipleship. These chapters are most suitable for lay readers and for church study groups.

The four chapters of part two will be of interest to ministers and scholars. These chapters treat the history of church discipline and some of the problems church discipline has encountered, especially in Protestantism. Part two is not, however, inaccessible to the average reader.

Loren Johns has kindly arranged questions for teachers and study groups who wish to use them in a study of this book. These questions are to be found at the back of the book.

PART 1

1

THE MANDATE
FOR DISCIPLING
"The Keys of the Kingdom"

*Evangelism and church discipline
are both acts of discipling.*

The basic New Testament text on church discipline is Matthew 18:15-18. The church has always considered it important partly because it represents the word of Christ and partly because it offers systematic instruction on the subject. Because of its importance both historically and for the subject of this book, the passage merits quotation here in full.

> If your brother sins against you, go and tell him his fault, between you and him alone. If he listens to you, you have gained your brother. But if he does not listen, take one or two others along with you, that every word may be confirmed by the evidence of two or three witnesses. If he refuses to listen to them, tell it to the church; and if he refuses to listen even to the church, let him be to you as a Gentile and a tax collector. Truly, I say to you, whatever you bind on earth shall be bound in heaven, and whatever you loose on earth shall be loosed in heaven.

We should examine this passage together with Matthew 16:18-19, where Peter confesses Jesus as "the Christ." In response Jesus says,

> You are Peter, and on this rock I will build my church.... I
> will give you the keys of the kingdom of heaven, and whatever
> you bind on earth shall be bound in heaven, and whatever you
> loose on earth shall be loosed in heaven.

John 20:22-23 is a third closely related text. In that passage
the risen Christ breathes upon the gathered disciples, saying,
"Receive the Holy Spirit. If you forgive the sins of any, they are
forgiven; if you retain the sins of any, they are retained."

These texts have shared a long association in the history of
interpretation and as a group have been the church's claim to
what former theology called the "power of the keys." Do these
passages provide a basis for church discipline? If so, what is the
nature of the discipline they support?

We have all heard jokes about people meeting St. Peter at
the pearly gates and awaiting an uncertain fate. Such stories are
the remnants of a long and strong church tradition. For many
centuries almost all Western Christians believed that Peter and
his alleged successors, the popes, controlled their eternal
destiny.

This traditional medieval interpretation of the power of the
keys held that the life of people in this world as well as their
destiny in the next was subject to the will of ecclesiastical
princes. The promise of Matthew 16:18-19 and 18:15-18 that
what was bound or loosed on earth would be bound or loosed
in heaven was considered a divine commitment to back up the
authority of the church. The church took this promise to apply
not only to spiritual matters but also to secular power. Thus all
through the Middle Ages many people lived in mortal fear of
what they considered the church's control over their bodies and
souls.

The Reformation called into question the church's alleged
authority over people's bodies and souls. A representative
Protestant criticism of the misinterpretation of the power of the
keys is that of Bullinger:

Many fancy things are said about the keys of the Kingdom of God, which were handed over to the apostles by the Lord. People forge from them swords, spears, scepters, and crowns and gain omnipotence over the greatest kingdoms, as well as over body and soul. Our opinion about this is based simply on the Word of the Lord, and we say that all properly called servants of the church possess the keys of the Kingdom of heaven and exercise the power of the keys when they proclaim the gospel.[1]

Similarly Calvin held that

this command concerning remitting and retaining sins, and that promise made to Peter concerning binding and loosing, ought to be referred to nothing but the ministry of the Word.... For what is the sum of the Gospel, but just that all being the slaves of sin and death, are loosed and set free by the redemption which is in Christ Jesus, while those who do not receive and acknowledge Christ as deliverer and redeemer are condemned and doomed to eternal chains.[2]

Menno Simons held the same view:

There are two heavenly keys.... The key of binding is nothing but the Word ... of God ... by which all are included under ... the wrath of God ... who do not by faith receive Christ....

The key of loosing is the abundantly cheering and delightful Word of grace ... and liberating Gospel of peace by which are delivered from ... the wrath of God those who with regenerated ... and believing hearts receive Christ and His Word....[3]

Protestant Reformers objected to the notion that in the promise of the keys God had written a blank check and surrendered his authority to the church. Thus Calvin claimed that in the promise of the keys "it is not so much power as ministry. Properly speaking, Christ did not give this power to men but to his Word, of which he made men the ministers."[4] The power of the keys was valid only if used in accordance with the direction of God's Word and Spirit.

Apostolic Succession

Modern biblical scholarship supports the Reformation interpretation of the "power of the keys." Some recent commentators still suggest that the rock refers to something other than Peter himself. However, we accept the statement made by Plummer already at the beginning of the century: "The first ten chapters of Acts show us in what senses Peter was the foundation on which the first stones of the Christian Israel were laid. . . . 'All attempts to explain the "rock" in any other way than as referring to Peter have ignominiously failed.' "[5] Barclay accepts this interpretation as the most natural one.[6] It is also the one Cullmann argues for in the book *Peter.*[7]

On this view the first ten chapters of Acts are the definitive commentary upon the meaning of Matthew 16:18-19. In Acts 1:15 Peter takes leadership among the 120. In 2:14 Peter preaches the Pentecost sermon. In 4:8 Peter takes leadership in the defense against the Sanhedrin. In 5:3 Peter again takes the lead in dealing with the Ananias and Sapphira scandal. In 8:14, 20 Peter has the primary role in the extension of the church to the Samaritans. In 10:34 Peter again takes the lead in opening the doors of faith for the first time to Gentiles. According to the biblical record, God assigned Peter a key role in establishing the messianic community.

This recognition of the primacy of Peter does not, of course, endorse the traditional Roman claims for the papacy. We must keep quite clear the distinction between Peter and Christ. It is Christ who says, "On this rock I will build my church." In the words of one commentator, "The church that Jesus founds upon Peter is his, Christ's church, and not Peter's."[8]

It would therefore be a serious misunderstanding to say, as Rome has in the past, "I am of Cephas" (see 1 Cor. 1:12). For Christ never surrendered his authority to Peter. Indeed, Peter exercised authority only by permitting himself to be an instrument used by Christ, the builder. Nonetheless, we cannot deny that Jesus granted Peter a historic foundational position in the church.

In the second place, we must keep clear the distinction between Peter and his successors. In the historic sense the apostle Peter is the one who opens the door of faith to both Jews and Gentiles. In that role he is unique and can have no successors. His place in the founding of the church can never be duplicated. What follows him is no longer foundation but part of the house built *upon* the foundation.

In another sense, the apostle Peter *must* have apostolic successors: missionaries and evangelists, those who are sent (which is what the word *apostles* means). Through them the building of the church continues. Without them its founding and Peter's place in its founding both come to nothing. As one scholar puts it, "The Apostle has, in fact, successors, namely, the whole church. As the apostolic church it succeeds to the authority to teach, though in such a way that it must always listen to what Peter says."[9]

The Power of the Keys

We can now examine the meaning of the metaphor of the keys and of the authority to bind and loose. The figure of keys is in keeping with the Old Testament image of the people of God as a temple or house. In Matthew 23:13 Jesus charges the Pharisees with shutting people out of the kingdom of heaven, which implies their custodianship of the door of faith. So the statement by Jesus in Matthew 16:18-19 was a familiar one to the Jewish mind of the day. To be invested with the keys of the kingdom was to be charged with the positive task of opening the doors of salvation to all who believed. This implied also the negative task of endorsing the exclusion from salvation of those who did not believe.

The terms *bind* and *loose* have as their background the ancient practice of binding captives or prisoners. Kings of Judah were "bound" and taken into exile (2 Kings 25:7; 2 Chron. 36:6). Herod "bound" John the Baptist and put him in prison (Matthew 14:3). Saul (Paul) set out for Damascus to arrest Christians and bring them "bound to Jerusalem" (Acts 9:2). Peter in prison was "bound with two chains" (Acts 12:6). And at the end of his life the apostle Paul was himself "bound" in chains and taken prisoner to Rome (Acts 28:20).

Binding referred literally, then, to the action of a religious or judicial authority in stopping illegal conduct. By extension it also came to refer figuratively to the act of proscribing certain behavior or declaring it impermissible.

Conversely, to loose meant literally to set prisoners free. Figuratively, it meant authoritatively to pronounce a given kind of conduct legal, ethical, and permissible.

By the time of Jesus the terms *bind* and *loose* had this established rabbinic use. Their primary meaning was, in fact, rabbinic declaration concerning what was forbidden or permitted in given applications of the law. Rabbinic rulings thus provided Jewish people guidance in their community's life. The words about binding and loosing may be interpreted as a parallel to the words about the keys. In the Christian context the authority to bind and loose is the commission to proclaim the gospel. It is the "rule of Christ," which leads people into righteousness, into the life of the kingdom. It also confirms the unrighteousness and consequent bondage of those who reject it.

The Great Commission

We propose that Matthew 16:18-19 does not deal with the subject of church discipline as traditionally understood. In the earliest tradition of the church, this text referred to the evangelistic mission of the church. Especially if one accepts Acts 1—10 as the definitive commentary upon Matthew 16:18-19, the power of the keys here signifies the opening of the door of faith to both Jews and Gentiles. The authority of binding and loosing similarly signifies the ethical governance of the messianic community. Matthew 16:18-19 thus contains what we could appropriately call an anticipation of the great commission.

This observation is supported by John 20:19-23. A parallel to Matthew 16:18-19, this passage is clearly a form of the great commission, not only because its context is the appearance of the risen Lord but also because of the elements in the account itself. There is first the gift of the Holy Spirit and the missionary mandate: "As the Father has sent me, even so I send you."

Then follow the words on remission and retention of sins. These words recall the Lucan version of the great commission, "that repentance and forgiveness of sins should be preached . . . to all nations" (Luke 24:47). They also recall Peter's words on the day of Pentecost, "Repent, and be baptized . . . in the name of Jesus Christ for the forgiveness of your sins" (Acts 2:38).

If Matthew 16:18-19 is an anticipation of the great commission, how are we to read the words in Matthew 18:15-18 about going to the sinning brother? For in this latter text the "going" is clearly to someone within the community of disciples, not to unbelievers. Yet in this text Jesus still speaks of the function of binding and loosing. The use of the same terms suggests that the commission to address a sinning believer is parallel to the great commission.

The relation of these texts clearly rests on more than the mere coincidence of certain words. There is a common task intended in these texts. The basis for incorporating people into the church is also the basis for discipline within the church. Since the church is founded upon the gospel, entrance into the community and continued life within it rest upon the same foundation. Hence the method proposed in Matthew 18 for dealing with sinners in the community is nothing other than that spelled out in Matthew 16 and John 20 for bringing sinners into the community.

To put it another way, the keys of the kingdom—or the authority to bind and loose—define the conditions for entrance into the kingdom. But more, they also define the ethical norms of life in the community. There is not one kind of binding and loosing in evangelism or missionary proclamation, but another in church discipline. In both situations the power of the keys and the commission to bind and loose represent the good news. They announce the coming of Christ's reign and its power to open the door to life under the rule of God.

Evangelism and church discipline are both acts of discipling. They are parallel or analogous ministries. Both have the same goal. Both seek the liberation of people from sin in all its forms to bring them into the way of Christian love, justice, peace, and joy. Both use the same method: the Word of God and the power of the Spirit.

The Ministry of Discipling

Too often in the history of the church the meaning of the gospel, though recognized in missionary proclamation, has been forgotten when it comes to discipline. Then the church has taken another track: charges, courts, trials, condemnation, punishment—in short, legalism and casuistry. We forget that what meets people initially as good news always remains the good news of the power of God's grace. It frees them from sin in order that they might live in conformity with God's gracious intention for humankind.

We can cite illustrations from church history that reveal this inconsistency between evangelism and discipline. Some past Protestant theologians, because of the plural of the term *keys,* distinguished between the key of doctrine and the key of discipline. They claimed the key of doctrine signified warning or admonition by the Word and the key of discipline admission to or exclusion from the outward privileges of the church. According to one Scottish churchman,

> The former [key] reaches to the thoughts and heart, and judges them, while the latter [key] is intended only to restrain, regulate, and judge the outward man.... By the key of doctrine was meant the preaching of the Word (including private admonition, counseling, and instruction, as well as [the] sermon ...) and the administration of Sacraments. The key of discipline ... was more commonly restricted to the infliction of various censures of the church and their removal.... In the use of the key of discipline the church condemns or approves only a man's outward practice; that is why its condemnation or approval can be absolute. It does not pretend to open or close the gates of heaven to any individual. ... On the other hand, the key of doctrine absolutely debars from the saving promises and, on condition of faith and true, inward repentance, absolutely opens the gates of heaven. Saving grace is the condition of absolution in the exercise of the key of doctrine; serious profession, outward decency, is the condition of absolution in the exercise of the key of discipline.[10]

The quotation clearly brings out an unfortunate distinction, well illustrated in the accounts given of Scottish church discipline. Membership in the church and its "saving promises" was—in theory at least—definitely "on condition of faith and true, inward repentance." However, discipline in the church—"the infliction of various censures"—was on the basis of "serious profession and outward decency."

Thus the Scottish church could send the sheriff after people who did not voluntarily attend "sabbath" worship. Or it could pillory in the vestibule of the church offenders not conforming to the church's moral standards. Such practices were hardly consistent with Calvin's claim that the power of the keys was a matter of the Word of the gospel alone.

A similar inconsistency appears in a popular modern biblical commentator, William Barclay. In view of the Protestant reinterpretation of the power of the keys in Matthew 16 and of the authority to remit sin in John 20, it is somewhat startling to discover in Barclay a continuing hang-up about Matthew 18. Barclay contrasts Matthew 18 rather sharply with Matthew 16.

Matthew 18:15-18, says Barclay,

> does not ring true; it does not sound like Jesus; it sounds much more like the regulations of an ecclesiastical committee than it does like the words of Jesus Christ. . . . It is far too legalistic to be a saying of Jesus . . . . The passage speaks of tax collectors and Gentiles as irreclaimable outsiders. Jesus was in fact accused of being the friend of tax-gatherers and sinners, and he never spoke of them as hopeless outsiders; He always spoke of them with sympathy and love, and even with praise. . . . The whole tone of the passage is that there is a limit to forgiveness, that there comes a time when a man may be abandoned by his fellow-men as beyond hope, a piece of advice which it is impossible to think of Jesus as having given. And the last verse, which deals with binding and loosing, actually seems to give the Church the power to retain and to forgive sins. There are many reasons which make us think that this, *as it stands*, cannot be a correct report of the words of Jesus, and that it must be an adaptation of something which He said, made by the Church in later days, when Church discipline was rather a thing of rules and regulations than of charity and forgiveness.[11]

But after making these criticisms Barclay says, "Although this passage is not a correct report of what Jesus said, it is equally certain that it goes back to something Jesus did say. Can we then press behind it and come to the actual commandment of Jesus?" In his commentary Barclay does not, however, try to recover this suggested "actual commandment of Jesus." Instead he merely reverses his attitude about the present text in Matthew. From it Barclay gives a good sketch of discipline according to the gospel—"a scheme of action for mending broken relationships within the Christian fellowship"![12]

But why then Barclay's original criticisms? In the interpretation of Matthew 16:18-19 the terms *bind* and *loose* give Barclay no difficulty. They refer to Peter's "administration of the church," as we see from Acts. Yet here they denote an apparently impossible "power to retain and to forgive sins."

Barclay's ultimately positive attitude toward Matthew 18:15-18 shows that the problem is not the wording of the passage nor whether this is a "correct report of what Jesus said." Rather, the issue is whether these words have been rightly understood in much of the history of the church. For on Barclay's own second interpretation, we can accept these words with no difficulty as a "correct report."

One suspects that prejudices against Matthew 18:15-18 such as those in Barclay's initial criticism represent an understandable reaction to centuries of abuse of the passage by legalistic interpretation and practice. This calls for disabuse of the passage, however, not a perpetuation of the misinterpretation. People such as Barclay still labor under unnecessary misconceptions if Matthew 16:18-19 means for them entrance into the community of faith by the gospel, while Matthew 18:15-18 implies the tyranny of ecclesiastical legalism.

There is, after all, only one kind of Christian existence. If there were two, then there might be one answer for the problem of sin in the non-Christian (the liberating power of the gospel) but another for the problem of sin in the Christian (the punishment of the law). Fortunately, there is only one gospel, which alone is the totally adequate answer for sin wherever it is found. The consequence of this is that we must undertake evangelism and church discipline in the same way. We declare the gospel in order to bring people into the way of Jesus Christ, to keep them in that way and, if necessary, to restore them to that way.

Have you ever heard of a ministry of evangelism that tried to bring people into the church by censuring some, withholding communion from others, ostracizing still others, as though such penalties would bring them to faith? Doesn't evangelism mean inviting all people to receive the new Christ nature and thereby to cross over into the new humanity? Church discipline is quite simply a continuation of that ministry.

We are paralleling discipline here with authentic evangelism, of course. This evangelism is more than religious TV or a religious Disneyland. It is more than a sensational experience. We mean by *evangelism* the process of delivering people from sin and integrating them into a responsible life of righteousness, power, freedom, and love in Christ's community. Such an evangelism makes disciples, baptizing them and teaching them to observe all things that Christ has commanded (Matt. 28:20).

The purpose of this book is to reinterpret the doctrine of church discipline in Matthew 18:15-18 and to place it once more in the context of the gospel. It is to liberate Matthew 18:15-18 from the legalistic interpretation it has suffered since medieval times. In the following pages we will explore each stage of the disciplinary process. We will constantly refer to the principle that discipline, like evangelism, is an act of discipling and as such a function of the gospel. By this method we hope to arrive at an evangelical doctrine of church discipline.

2

THE OCCASION
FOR DISCIPLING
"If Your Brother Sins"

*The occasion for church discipline is
a recognition of the peril of unfaith.*

According to Matthew 18:15 (and the parallel in Luke 17:3)
the mission of going to regain a fellow believer is prompted by
the notice of sin. "If your brother sins against you, go to
him. . . ."

The words sound simple enough, yet for many people they
do not seem to be a sufficiently clear guideline. What kind of
situation warrants the initiation of discipline? Peccadillos such
as overeating or stealing an apple?

These are not idle questions. The history of Christianity
shows alternating tendencies, the church sometimes becoming
obsessed with trivia, sometimes overlooking serious faults.[1]

A Catalog of Sins

Many writers in the history of Christianity have attempted to
compile a catalog of sins that offers a reliable guide for when to
initiate church discipline. Some have even sought to establish a
graduated scale of sins that automatically triggers the appropriate response from the church. Thus when a person commits
a certain sin, the church needs only to classify it to know how to
put its machinery in motion.

These writers speak of sins as petty, serious, grave, flagrant, notorious, or heinous. This suggests a scale of degrees of moral transgression, as though there is some line of seriousness at which the church begins the process of discipline. Unfortunately, the use of such a graduated scale usually leads the church to tolerate some sins but not others.

One writer has considered 1 Corinthians 5:11 and 6:9,11 to be an enumeration of

> the sins which demand excommunication of the offender: immorality, greed, idolatry, reviling, drunkenness, and robbery.... In another letter, an entirely different list of sins is given, perhaps "venial sins." These are "quarreling, jealousy, anger, selfishness, slander, gossip, conceit, and disorder." These Paul rebukes though he does not immediately threaten excommunication.[2]

One might comment that if such a distinction were helpful, it would still be necessary to decide when a given act was, for example, selfishness (second list) or greed (first list). However, the New Testament writers clearly did not intend us to use these lists of sins for this kind of distinction. First Corinthians 5:11 could hardly be a definitive list of those who are to be put out. This might leave a thief or murderer in communion, since theft and murder are not in Paul's list here. Surely Paul's list is simply a timely sample in a given situation.

Others have attempted to distinguish sins calling for excommunication from sins that presumably leave people in the church. These persons have collated and generalized from New Testament references to establish a type of legal precedent or casuistry. According to this method, says one writer, the New Testament justifies separation on moral or doctrinal grounds. Another claims the New Testament presents three grounds for exclusion of offenders: disruption of the fellowship, flagrant immorality, and denial of the faith. Another cites three classes of sinners who must be expelled: those who live in "open sin," those who cause divisions, and those who teach false doctrine.[3] Schism, heresy, and immorality seem to be the categories that emerge from this collation and generalization. These categories remind one of the early church's list of three mortal sins: murder, apostasy, and adultery.

The twofold classification of sins—those that call for excommunication and those that do not—hints at a valid principle of the gospel. Unfortunately, however, it draws an invalid conclusion. It infers that a certain class of sins in themselves cause a fall from grace and that therefore an individual's spiritual status can be prejudged. With this given class of sins the church can then bypass the invitation to repentance as unnecessary, for in effect these sins are by definition unforgivable. The corollary implication is that another class of sins is tolerable in that they do not require excommunication. The tendency to classify sins in this fashion usually leads to the inflexible condemnation of some sinners and the toleration of other sinners—even impenitent ones—in the church.

Calvin, for example, in dealing with the discipline of ministers explicitly distinguishes between "intolerable offenses" and "tolerable faults." "Intolerable offenses" led to "immediate deposition from the ministry as well as [to] . . . civil penalties." These offenses included blasphemy, simony, prolonged absence from duty, drunkenness, and dancing. "Tolerable offenses" deserved only fraternal reproof. These offenses included neglect of the study of Scripture, slander, quarreling, and anger.[4]

A little reflection persuades us that this common method of classifying sins only leads church discipline astray. On the one hand, a person might promptly and sincerely repent of so-called flagrant acts of sin. So the mere act of committing them does not call for excommunication. On the other hand, a person who is impenitent about what might be considered a trivial sin can end in that total loss of spiritual life that calls for exclusion from the community of faith.

To understand this principle one should note the analogous case of a non-Christian. Big sins are not an obstacle to an unbeliever's repentance and faith. Fortunately, most churches realize that bringing unbelievers to faith in evangelism is not a matter of measuring sins according to some scale. They know that big sins are not an obstacle to getting into the church—if there is repentance and faith. On the other hand, it takes only small sins to keep a non-Christian from salvation who refuses to repent. The condition for becoming a Christian in the first place is repentance and the reception of new life in Christ. Similarly, in church discipline the decisive test is simply repentance and faith.

Forgivable and Unforgivable Sin

If faith is such a decisive consideration—the great divide in church discipline as well as in evangelism—then we are dealing, it would seem, with only two categories. It is an instructive exercise to trace in the history of Christendom the development of this propensity to classify sins as venial and mortal, that is, forgivable and unforgivable.

Quite early in the history of the church the term *mortal* came to designate three specific sins or areas of sin. These were apostasy (idolatry), immorality (adultery or fornication), and murder. *Mortal* meant "unto death"—spiritual death. Unless one defined apostasy so broadly as to include everything not covered by immorality or murder, this threefold classification already leaves out broad classifications of sin—for example, the greed and lying of which Ananias and Sapphira were condemned.

Along with the restriction of mortal sin to these three categories came the practice of regarding them automatically as mortal, and even permanently mortal. Tertullian held that murder, idolatry, fraud, denial of Christ, blasphemy, adultery, fornication, and every other violation of the temple of God "admit of no pardon. . . . For these Christ will no longer plead;

these, he who has been born of God will absolutely not commit, as he will not be a son of God if he has committed them."[5]

There is no reason to conclude from a reading of the New Testament that a lapse such as Peter's denial of Christ, while certainly incompatible with life in the body of Christ, inevitably called for excommunication from the church. However, some church leaders in the second, third, and fourth centuries acted as though such a lapse inevitably required either permanent or temporary excommunication. If the church ever adopted an ironclad rule that refused forgiveness for post-baptismal mortal sin, this practice did not continue for long.

In due time the Catholic Church developed its full-dress system of penance. It claimed the authority to forgive even the so-called mortal sins—apostasy, adultery and murder—if there was genuine repentance. The history of confessional procedure in the third and fourth centuries seems to show that the church was concerned in some sense for evidence of genuine repentance and confession.

It apparently was not concerned enough, however. For just as the three major sins became automatically mortal (i.e., unforgivable) as shown by the rigorous rule of excommunication for mortal sin, so they later practically became automatically venial (i.e., forgivable) simply by expiation through penance. Thus three, nine, twelve, or twenty-seven years of penance apparently automatically secured forgiveness—at least according to the various penitential books that eventually came into use.

To be sure, allowances were made. Thus Gregory's penitential allowed that the "disposition of the party is to be of principal account."[6] Furthermore, public confession continued for a while, suggesting a lingering twilight of the primitive conception of a church discipline according to the gospel.

However, the disposition of the party was not of *decisive* account and shortened sentences were *exceptions* to the rule.

This causes us to doubt the genuineness of this apparent element of grace. On the whole the church recognized "a gradation of penalties suited to the character of the offenses."[7]

The misconception arose with the definition of *venial* and *mortal* as degrees of sin rather than as attitudes of the sinner. The church came to define sin in terms of a judicial scale and in terms of crime and punishment instead of in terms of grace and faith. Mortal sins were grave moral acts of transgression as defined by canon law. Mortal sin was no longer, as in the New Testament, sin the church was not able to forgive simply because of an offender's impenitence. With the advance of the Constantinian era the church adopted the legalism of the state and abandoned the principles of the gospel in coping with sin among its members.

The Unforgivable Sinner

Is there not, though, an unforgivable sin? Strictly speaking, there is not. Even if there were, it would not be necessary—or possible—to recognize such in advance. Nor would it make a difference in the initiation of disciplinary counsel. For it is precisely through the process of discipling that the church finds a person forgivable or unforgivable. Thus we should not speak of an unforgivable *sin* but only of an unforgivable *sinner*.

The essential nature of so-called unforgivable sin resides not in the quality of a given act but in the attitude of the sinner. It is not that God cannot or will not forgive certain acts. Rather, some individuals simply refuse to accept the invitation to repentance.

One writer in commenting upon pertinent passages in Hebrews (6:4-8; 10:26-27) expresses it this way: "Certain states of mind secure immunity from divine grace."[8]

A New Testament text dealing with this problem in the context of discipline is 1 John 5:16-18. Wescott gives an excellent interpretation of this passage, clarifying the meaning of *mortal sin* (RSV) or *the sin unto death* (KJV):

In the first and simplest sense a "sin unto death" would be a sin requiring the punishment of natural death (compare Numbers 18:22). . . . If now the same line of thought is extended to the Christian Society, it will appear that a sin which by its very nature excludes from fellowship with Christians would be rightly spoken of as a "sin unto death." We are not to think of specific acts, defined absolutely, but of acts as the revelation of moral life. . . . Death is, so to speak, its natural consequence, if it continue.[9]

We find help on the meaning of this passage from the story of Ananias and Sapphira (Acts 5:1-11). The sin of the offenders had literally mortal consequences. They forfeited their lives. Seen against this background, we must understand mortal sin as the loss of faith and its consequent spiritual death. It may be connected with a variety of sins or with no particular act of sin. It is more properly a state of mind.

We must interpret the text of 1 John 5:16-18 in the light of the foregoing explanations. The prayer mentioned in this text is the liturgical act of absolution. Not to pray for someone who has committed the mortal sin means not to pray the prayer of absolution over someone who has suffered spiritual death. The implication is that because of impenitence, the individual in question is not fit for restoration and should remain excommunicated. It does not imply unredeemable condemnation or even loss of concern for someone. In the words of Matthew 18 (note again the parallel with the Jewish ban), the church should regard that individual as a "Gentile and tax collector."

Strictly speaking, then, there are not even two kinds of sin, forgivable and unforgivable. There is only one kind, that described in the most basic terms as the absence of faith. We usually recognize this truth in evangelism, for there we do not deal with people according to whether they are guilty of given classes of sins. What matters there is the one essential mark of faith and spiritual life. Why is it so hard to see this principle when it comes to discipline?

"We should get away from considering church discipline a matter of sin and righteousness, but rather put it on the basis of faith and unbelief," says one writer.[10] Actually, discipline *is* a matter of sin and righteousness, but sin is essentially unfaith, and righteousness is faith. Sin is the rejection of the way of faith. Whenever one resorts to some list or catalog to define it, sin will be misunderstood and the practice of church discipline will become unchristian.

The criteria for recognizing the danger of a loss of faith or lapse from the discipled life are nothing other than the Word and Holy Spirit. That is, as the church undertakes its disciplinary task, it remains aware of the message of the whole New Testament. When used under the guidance of the Spirit, the New Testament adequately portrays the nature of life in Christ and by that token exposes the rejection of that life. Recognizing what kind of sin invites discipline is no easier or harder than recognizing what sin would prevent the baptism of someone who stands outside the church. In each case sin is ultimately an individual's refusal to follow the way of Christ.

The Problem of Secret Sin

Some have occasionally raised questions about the problems of secret sin. It is obvious that no one can act on something strictly unknown.

This does not, however, justify closing one's ears to reported sin and pretending it to be unknown. For such a matter is no longer secret. If the reporting is false or malicious, the church should deal appropriately with *that* problem.

One should not infer, further, that the church needs to act only on specific acts of sin. Not acting on dispositions and attitudes, such as greed and jealousy, implies that a person's spirit or attitude does not matter. Dispositions and attitudes often lead to specific acts of sin. Even if they do not, the attitudes themselves already affect the health of the church. As one writer puts it:

Sin, whether private or public, ought never to be considered a mere personal shortcoming. Not only does even the most secret sin create an attitude which disturbs the peace and the joy of the community, not only has it psychological consequences which shed abroad some degree of disorder and suffering; any sin, however secret, since it is the sin of the member of the body, is a drag on the Church because it causes a rupture in her relationship with God.[11]

So-called "secret sin" is not as big a problem as people in the church sometimes think. For one thing, the nature of the Christian life is such that persons cannot deceive themselves or others very long. Spiritual life is a potent reality that makes itself visible in a life of righteousness. Therefore, even if one conceals acts of sin, the symptoms of spiritual illness will surface somewhere. Some people have the mistaken notion that sin is the positive reality and righteousness merely an absence of acts of sin. Actually, it is the other way around. Spiritual life is the positive reality, and sin, being its absence, is the negative. Usually a person's spiritual condition is therefore fairly discernible.

In yet one other respect the problem of secret sin is not as problematic as often thought. Corresponding to the power of the gospel to manifest itself in spiritual life is its power to give the gift of discernment. We see this gift of the Spirit to discern the thoughts and intents of the heart in the New Testament church. We see it, for instance, in Acts 5 (the story of Ananias and Sapphira), Acts 8:21, and 13:10. In 1 Corinthians 14:25 Paul speaks of the "disclosure" of the secrets of people's hearts. As one interpreter puts it, "Paul knows of a *charisma* which he calls 'the ability to distinguish between spirits' (1 Corinthians 12:10 f.). . . . This *charisma* constitutes therefore a presupposition of discipline."[12]

It is not the church, then, but the person who is trying to hide sin who has the real problem. Secret sin usually has a way of exposing itself. Usually those trying to hide their sin are the most self-deceived in thinking they have kept it covered. There is no need for the church to resort to detective work to spy on sinners.[13]

Where the revealing signs of sin make their appearance, the church is constrained to approach the individual in question with the offer of help. This is not a matter of prying into the private lives of people. It is an attempt to help them return to the way of faith. If church discipline becomes a game of hide-and-seek, we have clearly lost sight of the meaning of discipling, for discipling is what the Christian cause is all about.

So the church does not go around looking for hidden sins. As in evangelism, so in discipline the church goes looking for discipleship, which by its nature is open and visible. Where discipleship is missing, there the church has the privilege and responsibility of offering people the gospel. The gospel is a "dynamic" force in the lives of people, calling them to a response (Rom. 1:16). It allows no neutrality and will inevitably receive its response, if not the obedience of faith, then the refusal of faith. In each case the response engenders its consequences in the character and lifestyle of the individual being confronted by the call to discipleship. Thus the best way of dealing with the problem of secret sin is simply the continued faithful teaching of the gospel and faithful action where any sin appears that threatens spiritual life and health.

There is no possibility of compiling a complete and final catalog of sins that invite disciplinary action. As stated above, discipline may be occasioned by a person's coldness of heart and neglect of Christian fellowship. On the other hand, discipline may not be necessary where immediate repentance shows that an individual has not experienced a fall from grace.[14]

Preventive Counsel

Identifying loss of faith—or the danger of it—as the occasion for discipline does not rule out other kinds of counsel. One need not hesitate to go to offenders until they have gone far down the road into spiritual distress. One may go to a fellow believer at any time and for any cause, provided it is in the right spirit and shows loving Christian discretion. Such is merely the regular and tactful mutual counsel in the faith that several writers call preventive discipline.[15]

For example, the church can and should give a person with a temper problem counsel on how to overcome this fault, even if that problem is not an immediate danger to the person's spiritual life. Nor does one need to wait until the perpetration of some gross transgression. Too often in the past church discipline has been preoccupied with so-called serious transgressions and has not had enough concern for the general spiritual health of believers. Too often, also, the church has drawn an artificial line between formal acts of church discipline and other processes of spiritual counsel. In the end they all have as their goal the discipled life, and in many cases timely spiritual counsel can forestall the loss of faith.

At the same time, and paradoxically, one doesn't have to go to a fellow Christian over every failing. "If Christians began cracking down on each other for any and every fault listed in Scripture, the result might be constant nit-picking and faultfinding rather than the building up of one another in the faith."[16] Moreover, "not all differences of belief or interpretation call for disciplinary action."[17] In their zeal otherwise well-intentioned Christians sometimes confront their fellow Christians over matters of taste or custom. There is the danger of trying to bring others into conformity with *one's own* views rather than into conformity with the image of Christ.

Though the church must not become tied to a particular catalog of sins, it should, like Paul in 1 Corinthians 5 and 6, be ready to identify quite specifically in a given historical or cultural context conduct incompatible with the Christian life. Luther once threatened to excommunicate a man who intended to sell a house for 400 Gulden that he had purchased for 30. Inflation had sent prices up, but the profit this man intended to rake off was exorbitant. Luther rightly labeled this piece of greed a sin that called for discipline.

> Congregations may at times have the duty to legislate behavior, but . . . they must be sensitive to the Holy Spirit both in regard to biblical principles and to changing social climates. . . . The question is a tricky one, but it cannot and should not be evaded. [18]

It is certainly appropriate to identify specific sins or types of sin that should receive the church's attention. However, the church must not arbitrarily use these to predetermine any given case. In fact, it is important and necessary for the church to review its definitions of sin periodically in order to avoid developing blind spots or distorted ethical vision.

It is also important that the church's concern not merely reflect conformity to prevailing cultural values. Often the church has become preoccupied with a limited aspect of life, such as doctrinal formulations, clothing fashions, or hairstyles. At the same time the church may neglect weightier matters such as schismatic behavior, greed, and economic injustice. Sometimes the values of secular law have influenced the church's judgment. Then the church's actions may simply endorse the biases of criminal justice, condemning people already condemned by the law. Or the church may excuse itself from exercising discipline in certain cases on the ground that persons have already been punished by the law. Then the church may neglect to reach out to such people with help. The church must take pains to shape its values by Scripture and the guidance of the Spirit.

We may now return to the question of what kind of sin should prompt the initiation of the emergency spiritual care we are discussing in this book. The occasion for church discipline is any sign of danger to a fellow believer's spiritual life or health.

"If your brother sins, go to him." He may already have repented, he may repent in response to admonition, or he may refuse to repent. In any case, *a recognition of the peril of the loss of faith prompts the initiation of the ministry of discipline.* The church cannot determine in advance where such an initiated procedure will lead. That is the reason for the process prescribed in Matthew 18:15-18.

3

THE METHOD OF DISCIPLING
"Go Reprove Him"

The church's approach in the ministry of discipline,
whether it is called admonition, exhortation,
rebuke, reproof, correction, or any other term,
must be a presentation of the gospel.

The instructions given in Matthew 18 for initiating church discipline say, "If your brother sins against you, go and tell him his fault, between you and him alone. If he listens to you, you have gained your brother."

Luke says more tersely, "If your brother sins, rebuke him," or, as the heading of this chapter suggests, "Go reprove him" (Luke 17:3).

Who Should Go?

It is possible to quibble about who is responsible to approach an offender according to certain words in this text: "If your brother sins *against you*" (emphasis added). Surely the occasion is not merely one of personal insult, as though we otherwise might not have to go. The case may not be unlike that of coming upon an accident victim. Anyone who happens to be present and aware of the tragedy will do what anyone should do in a similar situation: offer help.

Most Christians would accept the claim that *somebody* should go to the fellow believer in trouble. If those who know about the sin do not feel able to do so, then they should certainly not gossip about the problem. Nor should they ignore the problem in the name of privacy or personal freedom. Instead, they should go to responsible leaders in the church. Neglect is not excusable on any grounds.

The question of who should go to the offender often focuses on the issue of whether such counseling is the special responsibility of ordained ministers or also of lay people. At times the tendency has been for the church to place this task upon ministers, and often ministers have willingly or unwillingly accepted it as their special responsibility. Now, ministers often have special training, skills, or gifts for such counseling, but they do not have a privileged status or authority that makes church discipline their preserve. Generally, the making of disciples is not usually considered the prerogative of the clergy.

The summons to go to an erring believer is not just a suggestion. It is a command.[1] It is an imperative of the same order as the great commission of Matthew 28:19: "Go ... make disciples of all nations ... teaching them to observe all that I have commanded you." This text makes no distinction between clergy and laity. The great commission is for the whole church.

The approach to someone in spiritual trouble has most commonly been called admonition. Titus 3:10 speaks of one or two admonitions, but some traditions speak of a "threefold admonition." This perhaps follows the directions of Matthew 18 to use three stages in a disciplinary proceeding.

The directions for initiating discipline seem simple enough. Unfortunately, this is what has raised a problem for many Christians. The directions are too simple, some think, because they do not seem to take into account the complexities of different situations. Sometimes admonition is considered too severe, sometimes too lenient. And so the church has vacillated between lenience and severity through much of its history.

Immediate Excommunication
Some writers have argued that the instructions about admonition are not applicable in certain situations. The church can

then lay them aside and excommunicate immediately. Those who would argue thus may claim to find biblical precedent for this. They might cite Acts 5, in which Peter apparently does not pause to admonish Ananias and Sapphira, and 1 Corinthians 5, in which Paul discourages further delay in the excommunication of the immoral man.

One can also find precedent for immediate excommunication in the history of the church. According to an early church document called the Apostolic Constitutions, the postapostolic church did not use the threefold admonition, at least not in cardinal sins. This document instructs the bishop to proceed as follows:

> When you see the offender in the congregation, you are to . . . give orders that he be expelled from it. . . . Then you shall order him to be brought into the Church; and after having examined whether he be truly penitent, and fit to be readmitted into full Communion, you shall direct him to continue in a state of mortification for . . . two, three, five, or seven weeks, according to the nature of the offense; and then after some proper admonitions, shall dismiss [or absolve] him.[2]

The order here—excommunication, then admonition—is the opposite of the instructions in Matthew 18. There Jesus instructs the church to excommunicate only if the brother or sister does not repent.

At the time of the Reformation some people held that the church could dispense with admonition in certain cases. According to the Anabaptist Peter Riedemann there were two classes of sins, "those which are a cause for admonition, and those which cause excommunication without admonition, these latter being fornication, covetousness, idolatry, railing, drunkenness, theft, and robbery."[3] This is, in effect, an expansion of the early church's list of mortal sins. Riedemann justified this by an appeal to 1 Corinthians 5 and 6.

Menno Simons early "made no distinction of sins" and

"spoke without differentiation of three admonitions." Later, however, he decided that in some cases it was "altogether improper . . . to run after [some] immoral wretches any longer with three admonitions before expulsion." He explained his reasoning. "With these three admonitions concerning gross offensive miscreants we would make many great hypocrites."[4]

A Puritan Congregational document takes the same view of the matter:

> But if the offence be more publick at first, and of a more heinous and criminall nature, to wit, such as are condened by the light of nature; then the Church without such graduall proceeding, is to cast out the offender.[5]

So the urge to bypass admonition and excommunicate immediately is not unusual in the history of the church. It is a strong urge, and its rationale is concern to guard the witness of the church and to prevent presumptuousness on the part of the sinner. The really serious danger to the church's witness, however, may be not the alleged seriousness of a person's sin, but the failure of the church to do something about it.

It would be strange indeed to consider admonition a toleration of sin when its intention is precisely the opposite—to call someone back to discipleship. Actually, hasty excommunication hurts the church's witness more, because people then come to regard the church as self-righteous, concerned more for its image than for the restoration of the erring. If an offender remains impenitent the church still has recourse to excommunication.

So church discipline must not bypass admonition. Every erring individual must be given an opportunity to repent and receive forgiveness. Only if it becomes clear that an offender rejects such an opportunity is excommunication warranted. And then exclusion from the church is on the ground of the rejection of that grace which offers to remove the person's guilt and redeem him or her from the power of sin.

What about 1 Corinthians 5? Likely Paul did follow the principle about admonition laid down in Matthew 18. The reference to his previous letter (1 Cor. 5:9-13) bears this out. Out of loving concern the offender mentioned in 1 Corinthians 5 was given ample opportunity to turn from his sinful way.

Naturally, some cases of discipline may proceed much faster than others if it quickly becomes obvious whether an individual is penitent or impenitent. So it is not necessary for the church's reputation to suffer from a long toleration of the impenitent.

Neglect of Admonition

In reaction to the judgmental attitude of the church in so much of its history, some have hesitated to speak the word of admonition at all. Was not Christ nonjudgmental in his association with sinners? Did he not say, "Do not judge, or you too will be judged" (Matt. 7:1,3, NIV)?

Some Christians refrain from going to an individual in spiritual trouble out of concern to follow what they think is the example of Jesus. Some refrain to avoid self-righteousness, to avoid mistaken judgment, or to keep from offending people and thereby doing more harm than good. They often propose that the right way to deal with sin in the church is to expect people to engage in self-discipline. All people, they hold, must resolve their own moral problems.

There is admittedly an element of judgment present already in an act of admonition, not only in an act of excommunication. It is the preliminary and tentative assessment that a given person's conduct or spirit is not in conformity with the Christian way. This initial assessment is subject to further check, as Matthew 18 teaches. The response of the person in question confirms or corrects this assessment. Furthermore, it is always subject to further review by "two or three witnesses," by the whole congregation, or even by a conference of congregations.

In any event, the kind of judgment implied in admonition is

in principle no different from the judgment implied in an act of evangelism or missionary proclamation. For evangelism also begins with tentatively judging someone to be in need of discipling, a judgment confirmed or corrected by the observed outcome.

To neglect admonition may *seem* to some members of the church to be the high road of not "judging" others. In fact it is the heartlessness of not offering help. The problem Jesus was trying to correct was a judgmentalism that made no room for grace. Refusing to offer the grace of release from sin is precisely like the neglect to make the grace of God available to unbelievers in evangelism. It is a misunderstanding of grace.

There is good reason not to neglect admonition. According to one pastor who interviewed several others, "When there is an effort made to effect change immediately after the sin comes to light, rarely is discipline by disfellowshipping necessary."[6]

Legalism Instead of Admonition

The most common tendency of the church in much of its history has been the development of a casuistry similar to that of secular law. This happens when the church places sins on a scale of severity and establishes a gradation in the penalties intended to deal with such degrees of sin. In this view, small sins merit admonition, slightly more serious sins perhaps public rebuke or censure, and still more serious sins suspension from communion. Grave sins deserve full excommunication and really heinous sins the anathema.

A Baptist discipline of 1774 speaks of "Church censures, which differ in their nature according to the nature and degree of the offense."[7] Similarly, one recent writer speaks of a "mild form" of discipline in which someone is "spoken to." In "more serious cases" the church invites people "not to take part in brotherhood meetings." In "very serious cases" the church tells a person "before the assembled brotherhood that he is excluded from all community of the common table, from all meetings, and from the inner peace of the Church."[8]

The church can and should, of course, make distinctions. An assault is admittedly more serious than shoplifting. It is important, though, that the church give attention to both cases in order to bring about repentance and transformation.

Further, the rediscipling efforts of the church are of the same character in both instances as they would be if the persons were unbelievers. Evangelism does not impose differing penalties according to the "degree of the offense." If the church's goal is persons "transformed by the renewing of [their] minds," then the approach must be the address of the gospel.

If the goal is merely social control, then the church must ask whether it has surrendered its proper mission. Even here, however, it is the gospel that has repeatedly done the better job of social transformation.

Admonition as an Appeal of the Gospel

It is true that the New Testament uses various expressions to describe the approach to an erring believer. The pastoral epistles speak of a *rebuke* (1 Tim. 5:20 and Titus 1:13; 2:15) or of a *correction* (2 Tim. 3:16). Some interpreters thus propose a complex judicial scheme like that just discussed. In this way they miss a most fundamental principle. *The initial approach in the ministry of church discipline—whether it is called admonition, exhortation, rebuke, reproof, correction, or any other term—must be a presentation of the gospel.*

We have said before that admonition of an erring believer is analogous to evangelism. As in evangelism repentance and faith issue in forgiveness and fellowship, so in discipline a positive response to the word of admonition issues in forgiveness and continued fellowship.

In evangelism the church respects an individual's rejection of the gospel and does not incorporate that person into the body of Christ. In a similar way, the church respects an individual's rejection of the word of admonition and formally recognizes that person's decision to no longer follow Christ. The difference is that admonition addresses a sinner in the church, while evangelism addresses one outside the church.

It is possible to have a formal observance of the threefold admonition that may not really proceed in the spirit of the gospel. Then the threefold admonition can degenerate into three stages of a trial calculated to establish guilt and pass sentence. Usually a sign of such a departure from the Christian spirit is the use of terms such as *filing charges, church court,* or *trial.*[9]

To be sure, beginning the process can be orderly, structured, and perhaps even formalized to some extent. The danger is that organization may frustrate the very purpose for which it was formed—namely, to present the claims of the gospel. Matthew 18:15 does not teach that the notice of sin should set grinding in motion the machinery of church discipline. It simply invites us to go to the person in trouble. Church discipline requires personal involvement and concern because the gospel is always a personal appeal. "If [someone] is overtaken in any trespass, you who are spiritual should restore him in a spirit of gentleness," writes Paul (Gal. 6:1).

This caution about the danger of legalism does not imply that the church is not concerned for the truth or for accuracy about the facts of a given case. Those undertaking church discipline must scrupulously avoid proceeding on false charges because of mere suspicion or hearsay.

At the same time, church discipline is something quite other than secret investigations or attempts to prove someone innocent or guilty. Admonition looks for the marks of true Christian life. If these are present, the truth about the details of a given case is no insuperable problem. If the marks of true Christian life are absent, there is little point in looking for the "facts." The fundamentally decisive fact is already clear.

As in evangelism, so also in discipline, there is only one

gospel. This is true whether people are guilty of so-called big or little sins. This gospel does not set out a schedule of penalties for a given code of sins but offers deliverance from sin as such. Repeated admonition seeks to ensure that no offender in the church is denied a clear invitation to continue in or to return to the way of faith. The church excludes no one except the person who in full awareness rejects such an offer.

It is sad to notice how absent this evangelical view of admonition has been in the history of the church. From time to time the church has been lenient, tolerating sin without admonition. Or it has excommunicated immediately without admonition. Or it has legalistically imposed "penalties suited to the offenses." None of these three alternatives is true to the gospel, because the gospel stands for the discipled life. Where church discipline is faithful to the gospel, it will unfailingly begin with admonition.

Confidentiality

Matthew contains an important principle in the instructions about speaking to an offender "between you and him alone." As Jay E. Adams helpfully points out, it is the principle of confidentiality.[10] To go to the individual means *not* to go to others with gossip.

The commitment to confidentiality dare not be absolute, however. For if the offending or transgressing individual does not repent, additional counsel must be brought into the case, perhaps eventually even the congregation. The promise of absolute confidentiality would prevent such wider involvement. Or, wider involvement would violate the promised confidentiality.[11] Of course, the wider involvement of additional counsel or of the congregation should also be confidential within those circles. The church has no interest in defaming people before society. It should understand that it operates by a different code than does public television, secular courts of law, or the *National Enquirer.*

Furthermore, a person is to carry a case forward to a higher level only because of impenitence or a "refusal to listen."[12] Otherwise, the matter stops at the level of private, personal encounter. In that sense the extent of knowledge depends upon the response of the person under discipline—unless the sin was public in the first place. The widening scope is not *for the sake of* an individual's public exposure. The wider involvement happens only as a consequence of the church's faithfulness in bringing the problem to resolution.

Two or Three Witnesses

Matthew 18 envisages the possibility of an offender responding negatively to the word of admonition and invites the concerned Christian to take "two or three witnesses" (KJV). This terminology comes from Jewish law. The account of the trial of Jesus illustrates how Jewish law required two witnesses for a conviction.

Bringing in additional counsel where necessary is not, however, merely to perpetuate an ancient Jewish custom or to secure a conviction. The purpose of additional counsel is, first, to assess the situation in general. It is to clarify the facts of a given case to prevent false charges. It is to discern the attitudes of both parties to ensure the problem is not some person's need to control others.[13] It is to prevent mere personality clash. And finally it seeks to determine whether the problem is indeed a matter of serious spiritual consequence.

Small-group consultation will also help to prevent hasty or biased action while providing a continued opportunity for a positive response. There may need to be a whole series of meetings of a small-group nature, perhaps with elders of the church, to reach clarification and a definite conclusion about the situation.

Furthermore, the use of "two or three witnesses" helps to confirm an individual's impenitence, if that is what it turns out to be. It is often the case, however, that individuals who resort to denial or try to bluff their way at the first private confrontation take the matter more seriously when confronted by several elders. Persuaded of the best course, these persons genuinely repent and are restored to Christian obedience.

Small-group effort also helps to make sure that the church's concern for an individual's restoration does not get stalled but moves forward to resolution. Too many cases bog down for lack of conscientiousness in moving cases to resolution. This lack of resolution is a harmful decision by default, for it neither presents the plea for penitence nor warns offenders against self-deceit in case of their impenitence.

Needed additional counsel should be chosen with care.

> Since these persons must offer counsel and possibly will become witnesses if that counsel is spurned, it would be wise . . . to call on persons who are best able to offer wise counsel and whose words of testimony, if needed, would be respected by the congregation.[14]

Individuals under discipline should themselves be permitted in appropriate circumstances to bring "witnesses." One writer advises, for example, that the church not require a woman to face a row of male church dignitaries. Securing witnesses dare not become a matter of lining up church pillars against a lone and hapless church member who is vulnerable to abuse of power in such a situation.[15]

Tell It to the Church

If the sinning person doesn't listen to the counsel of the witnesses, then "tell it to the church," advises Matthew 18:17. Two main points need to be noted about this third stage of the process. First, escalation does not signify any change in approach or spirit. The additional level of involvement does not signal a departure from a nonthreatening, compassionate, or gracious appeal. Official, structured, organized congregational action need not become impersonal, unloving, or unchristian.

Second, congregational presence and participation is essential at this stage because the issue has become nothing less than membership itself. This issue, like baptism, is by nature congregational, since it bears upon the relationship of every member of the congregation to the person under discipline. Therefore, when a case comes to this critical stage, the decision must contain the wisdom and carry the authority of the whole congregation. The whole congregation must be informed. There is a place for corporate, weighty decisions.

One question that comes up repeatedly in discussions of church discipline concerns how much time one should allow between the successive steps in the process. Jim Stafford reports a case in which the persistent, stubborn, and wearying struggle of a pastor over a period of weeks finally won out against the pressures of adultery and threat of divorce between two young couples. Several of the individuals involved had indicated that they wanted to remain Christian. This kept the pastor from giving up. His patience paid off.[16]

One theologian suggests that "too little time might result in procedures that [are] more punitive than restorative." He says it is important to give "ample time for repentance and change after each stage" of the disciplinary process.

> The chief criterion ... is the presence or absence of '*visible* progress, or *visible* responsiveness to admonition and rebuke.' If the offender is showing signs of softening as the Word of God is applied, time should be given for the Spirit of Christ to do His work.... If after a reasonable time the offender demonstrates an unrepentant attitude or hardening of heart, then those involved in the disciplinary process would be wise to move to the next step.[17]

A person under discipline should always have the choice of withdrawing or "resigning" from membership. Although that person should be apprised of the significance of such a decision, once made, the church must respect it. The act of withdrawing from membership in one sense effectively brings the case to a close. The congregation should know about such a resignation from membership.[18] Withdrawal from membership may or may not be regarded the equivalent of excommunication—that is, the loss of faith. Such an interpretation would depend in part upon the stage of the process at which it occurs, in part upon the church's discernment of the person's spirit and attitude at the time, and in part upon the motives for the withdrawal.[19]

"Frequently unrepentant persons change churches in order to avoid discipline . . . . In such a situation the receiving church [must] inquire about past church membership." Then "the former church [must state that] the person in question did not leave the church in good standing and that there are some concerns that have not been resolved."[20]

The teaching of Matthew 18 about going to an erring brother or sister is not about a rigid and inflexible process the church must follow slavishly. However, its principles deserve to be heeded well.

1. If some situation appears that signals a critical danger to someone's spiritual health or life, the church must reach out with help.

2. Concerned Christians must make repeated appeals to erring believers to accept the grace that can free them from the destructive effects of sin.

3. If necessary, the church must widen the sphere of examination and review. It must honestly recognize and respect the decisions of those who remain impenitent and abandon the Christian way.

The contemporary church might well give more attention to Matthew 18 and its summons to *go* deliver Christians caught by the power of sin. That is no less important a mission than to *go* and preach the gospel to unbelievers. As already shown, the ministry of discipling sinners in the church is a logical corollary of the mission of discipling all nations.

4

THE GOAL OF DISCIPLING
"If He Repents, Forgive Him"

*Forgiveness is the realization of the discipled life.
In discipline, as in evangelism, the church seeks
nothing more and settles for nothing less.*

Matthew 18:15 is quite brief in its description of the out-come of a disciplinary proceeding in which the word of admonition has been heeded. "If he hears you, you have gained your brother." The Luke 17:3 parallel is equally brief. "If he repents, forgive him." Thus the response desired by admonition would seem to be quite clear and uncomplicated.

However, the exact nature of the response sought in discipline has been the occasion of much debate in the history of Christianity. What are the marks of repentance? How can one determine the sincerity of a repentance? What is the place of confession? Should confession be public or private? What should such confession—public *or* private—include? What is the nature of the forgiveness sought in discipline?

Both texts carry the conditional *if*, and the subsequent verses of Matthew 18 elaborate upon the consequences of impenitence. Matthew recognizes the possibility that a person may not repent and receive forgiveness. The person may instead be excommunicated—treated "as a Gentile and a tax collector." The church is not to forgive automatically. The appropriateness of forgiveness depends on certain conditions.

A sense of this may have prompted Peter's question in Matthew 18:21, "Lord, how often shall my brother sin against me, and I forgive him? As many as seven times?" Jesus answers, "I do not say to you seven times, but seventy times seven." And yet in the parable of the unforgiving debtor following directly after these words to Peter (Matt. 18:23-35) Jesus depicts a situation in which forgiveness is not even granted twice, let alone seventy times seven times!

Two Views of Forgiveness

There are two distorted views of forgiveness possible, and the logic of each is not hard to follow. Those who forgive easily and endlessly do so to permit people to enjoy that unfailing mercy which can never be outlasted by sin. They believe such mercy will greet the sinner on the other side of every transgression. Those who forgive only once do so to prevent people from presumptuously taking advantage of grace in order to indulge in repeated sinning.

These alternatives are usually polarized against each other, each trying to avoid the pitfall of the other. The lenient alternative—unlimited toleration of sin—intends to avoid unrealistic demands for moral perfection. The severe alternative—setting a limit upon divine grace by refusing to excuse certain sins or refusing to forgive more than a given number of times—intends to avoid presumption.

When applied to church discipline, these two views of forgiveness express themselves in quite different approaches and objectives. Those who hold the lenient view usually hesitate to discipline at all. Whatever discipline they do engage in offers convenient absolution. Those who hold the strict view tend to engage in rigorous, even punitive discipline.

In the first view, the church grants forgiveness unconditionally because the goal is to magnify divine mercy in the face of what is expected to be inevitable human failure. In the second view, forgiveness is contingent upon moral reform because the goal is to take God's righteousness seriously.

One can observe these two respective views of forgiveness in the history of church discipline; first the severe, then the lenient. In most of the postapostolic and early Latin periods of church history, the church granted only one or two forgivenesses. A Christian who abused forgiveness through postbaptismal sin was not allowed further forgiveness, except perhaps a deathbed absolution. He was bound and not loosed "till he should pay all his debt" (Matt. 18:34). But with the advent of mandatory annual confession by the end of the Middle Ages, the church which claimed succession to Peter was listening to Christ's *other* word to Peter. The church was ready to offer forgiveness seventy times seven. And that led merely to indulgence.

The lenient view—seeing forgiveness as a toleration of sin— is a longstanding, popular, and harmful misconception in Western Christianity. It sees forgiveness as essentially dropping charges, "letting someone off," declining to impose any penalty for wrongdoing. It assumes that forgiveness represents a change in the forgiver instead of in the one forgiven. It is as though those who forgive—including in the first place, God— succeed in getting themselves to condone continued failure. In modern terms this is sometimes called "self-acceptance." The indulgent view of forgiveness leaves the sinner a sinner. It may intend to magnify divine mercy, but its actual effect is to denigrate the character and integrity of God and of the church. It insinuates that we do not need to take seriously God's call to righteousness.

It has been a bane of Western Christianity to see forgiveness as mere absolution without regard for ethical renewal. In American Christianity one attempt to remedy this defect in the understanding of forgiveness has been to posit a "second work of grace" or "baptism of the Spirit." This experience is to take believers beyond mere forgiveness into "victory" over sin. However labeled, this attempted remedy merely confirms and perpetuates the shortchanged conception of the so-called first work of grace. Forgiveness becomes bare absolution without moral renewal and power.

The other misconception of forgiveness is the strict or harsh or legalistic view, one that is inclined to demand punishment. Punishment, however, actually hinders repentance and forgiveness because it becomes a *substitute* for ethical transformation. Criminal offenders, for instance, assume their fine or prison stint "pays their debt to society" and excuses them from going to their victims and making right what they did wrong.

According to this thought, the penalty "makes up for" the offense. Therefore the offender need not address the problem of the sinfulness itself. At best, society's punishment of offenders is satisfied to curb external behavior without expecting to change the character or nature or motivation or values of the transgressor. To punish an offender hints that true repentance has not occurred. It may even signify that no one even asked for or expected repentance because the offender has had to pay instead.

An example of this misconception of forgiveness is a husband buying his wife a fur coat to make up for his adultery, or a woman punishing herself in some fashion for alcohol abuse, as though that might atone for the unresolved alcohol problem.

Note well that this punitive misconception of forgiveness, like the indulgent one, still permits an offender to remain unchanged. The very fact that people accept punishment as a *substitute* for change shows that they have resigned themselves to the individual remaining a sinner. So the problem with *both* indulgence and punishment is that they have given up on the prospect of transforming the sinner and have settled for chronic failure.

Authentic Forgiveness

It bears repeating. Rightly defined, understood, and practiced, forgiveness does *not* tolerate unrighteousness and failure.

Rather, it *achieves* righteousness through the power of the Word and Spirit of God as mediated through the resourceful, perceptive, and strong ministrations of the church.

Authentic forgiveness effectively remedies the problem of sin by changing the sinner. For example, it brings the thief to understand why theft is folly. It helps him understand what brought him to the act of theft, and what is needed to cease stealing. True forgiveness brings a formerly sinful person to a new mentality, attitude, and course of action. It creates the capacity to envisage and adopt a new pattern of behavior marked by self-respect and respect for others—in short, one of love and justice.

Understanding authentic Christian forgiveness helps us recognize its basic features and shows us how to forgive in quite specific ways in the discipling process.

First, such forgiveness is more than routine confession and absolution each Sunday morning. Parroting "we have done those things we ought not to have done," and receiving the responsive intonation, "if we confess our sins, he is faithful and just to forgive us our sin . . ." is not enough, profound and venerated as those words might be. Such a weekly recital does not really help an alcoholic, fornicator, or shoplifter. Unfortunately it may, in fact, subtly prevent such people from getting real help.

Can you imagine persons repeatedly confessing a violation of health rules? "We have broken the health rules again this week," they would say. "If we admit we have broken the health rules we will be forgiven." Indeed! What is needed is a doctor's explicit clarification of what is needed for the recovery of health.

Discipline for sin requires a similar *specific* address to the *specific* problem with *specific* counsel.

Second, forgiveness provides appropriate help for those needing it. Out of his several interviews Mark Littleton reports that

discipline is successful when there are follow-up and support for
those who have sinned. . . . The disciplinary procedure [is] not
simply a confrontation situation, but also a restoration process
in which the sinner [is] helped through counsel and support to
overcome his problem.[1]

Forgiveness is not a matter of lightly leaving some
transgression behind, everyone quickly turning the page on a
given failure. Meaningful forgiveness includes arranging
needed guidance for the person being forgiven.

Jay E. Adams draws attention to Paul's counsel to the Corinthians to restore someone. In reference to the phrase "forgive
and assist him" (2 Cor. 2:7), Adams says,

The word for "assist" is . . . variously translated in the New
Testament "comfort, help, assist, urge, persuade, counsel," . . .
literally, "to call alongside for assistance."

This assistance, or help, is too frequently missing in churches.
As a result, reinstated members make their way only with great
difficulty and may fall again into sin.[2]

This means effort, time, and whatever else may be required to
bring it about should be given . . . that the [restored bond] becomes stronger than it was before the break.[3]

Third, in line with the point just made, forgiveness can make
legitimate demands. It is not inconsistent with the gracious and
generous nature of forgiveness to require the person being forgiven to accept quite specific conditions for reshaping behavior.

In a case reported by Rev. Don Baker, a fellow pastor was
given—and required to receive as part of his forgiveness—
professional counsel on how to stay out of temptation and
danger.[4] Such demands are not forced upon someone but willingly embraced. They are thus not so much preconditions of

forgiveness as they are the substance of forgiveness itself. That is, they provide erring believers with the strategy to return to the way of righteousness. To make demands is not to revert to the righteousness of works. Rather, demands are the shape of the gift of grace because they represent the church's enabling assistance. True grace does not consist of empty words but strength-communicating acts that enable the overcoming of transgression.

Fourth, because forgiveness is not a toleration of continued sin but the realization of victory over sin, it *does* forego the demand for punishment. It remits the penalty. This is the "scandal" of the gospel of justification by grace through faith that Paul expounds in his letter to the Romans. The goal of God's law is righteousness, not punishment. The one legitimate purpose of punishment might be to achieve deterrence or reform—to turn an individual from sin. However, if repentance and forgiveness have already achieved the goal of turning the offender to righteousness, to punish at that point suggests some other objective than righteousness, perhaps to inflict pain and suffering out of a subtle desire for revenge.

Fifth, it is important for the church to use visible symbolic acts to communicate and convey that forgiveness. In conversion the church uses the symbol of baptism to mark the decisive crossing over from unfaith to faith. As a public rite, baptism communicates a power that a private and subjective decision on the street or in a coffee shop cannot. A new status, a new life, is a momentous event that calls for a liturgical rite to express it and effect it.

The early church formally forgave a penitent through the liturgical act of "the laying on of hands," usually during the Easter baptismal season. The restoration of penitent saints in discipline today should similarly use appropriate ways to assist recovenanting in the obedience of faith.

Sixth, there is a sense in which forgiveness decisively closes a case, even though it may well require the process of counsel just described. This is true precisely because forgiveness is not toleration of sin but the overcoming of sin and the realization of a new spiritual and moral state of affairs. It is not forgiveness if some past sinful act or life that a forgiven individual has really left behind is dredged up repeatedly or kept hanging over that person's head. Forgiveness is a celebration of a new life, for which reason it is not inappropriate to speak with Don Baker of moving "beyond forgiveness."

Forgiveness in the sense we have given that term means that spiritually debilitating acts and habits can in truth be put behind us, so that persons forgiven through a healing discipline can move on to joyful, free lives, self-respecting and respected by their Christian sisters and brothers. Such a life is as possible for disciplined saints as it is for sinners converted and baptized into the church in the first place.

Deeds of Repentance

Understanding the principles of forgiveness goes a long way toward answering some of the problems about repentance and confession raised in discussions of church discipline. Popular perception sees repentance essentially as a feeling. Repentance is "feeling bad" about a certain course of conduct and its consequences.

Rightly conceived, however, repentance is an act. Though strong feelings may quite appropriately be present, repentance is not just feeling sorry about what happened. It is not just feeling remorse about what one did, but discovering the insight and power to renounce that course of conduct and return to the Christian way. Repentance, properly defined, includes whatever measures are needed to turn one's pattern of life around. That includes the determination to seek reconciliation, restore relationships, and offer restitution where appropriate. The Bible speaks of "*deeds* of repentance."

On discerning the genuineness of a repentance, one theologian remarks "that genuine repentance will make itself evident by its deeds." He draws attention to the words of John the Baptist, who "told the multitudes to 'bring forth fruits in keeping with [their] repentance' " (Luke 3:8). Paul instructed the Gentiles to perform "deeds appropriate to repentance" (Acts 26:20).[5] Changing the behavior for which one is disciplined is the most important sign of genuine repentance.

Repentance does, of course, include honesty and sincerity. Biblical scholarship has always pointed out that repentance (*metanoia*) is a change of mind. It is deliverance from moral delusions. It is the recovery of 20/20 moral vision. Repentance may well include the jolting realization that one was indulging in games of self-deception.

That realization is possible only when one has come to see the truth. It's like the prodigal son of Luke 15 coming to his senses, realizing he did not need to live among the hogs. There *was* an alternative available. As this classic New Testament story of repentance shows, repentance provides the strength for amendment of life.

The Confession of Faith

The church has engaged in much debate throughout history over the role of confession in church discipline.

We must remember that the most fundamental meaning of confession in the New Testament is confession of faith. This meaning the apostle Paul expresses well in Romans 10:9-10.

> If you confess with your lips that Jesus is Lord and believe in your heart that God raised him from the dead, you will be saved. For [one] believes with his heart and so is justified, and he confesses with his lips and so is saved.

This confession has, of course, two aspects. The confession of faith by its nature implies also the confession of sin. To confess the way of Christ is to repudiate its opposite, the way of sin.

Confession of faith and confession of sin are inseparable. We can never have one without the other. To know the way of righteousness implies a recognition of its opposite, unrighteousness. And to recognize the way of sin as sin presupposes the recognition of righteousness, in the light of which one rightly recognizes sin for what it is. Of these two aspects confession of sin may be logically first, but recognition of sin becomes possible only when one becomes aware of the option of faith.

We can see the dual nature of confession in the experience of a new convert to the faith. The confession made is primarily a spontaneous and joyous confession of faith. This confession is not hidden but open—that is, freely made before all people. There is certainly present in this confession an acknowledgment of sin, because the first sign of spiritual life is honesty in recognizing former sinfulness. But the authentically Christian confession of a convert is not basically a recitation of past sins. It is a celebration of the new life in Christ.

The New Testament clearly projects this positive understanding of the meaning of confession. In the story of the lost sheep that was found, there is rejoicing over the sinner that repents. This passage precedes the one on discipline in Matthew 18 and ties in with the parable of the prodigal son in Luke 15. That case too ends in rejoicing.

The sinner, we must remember, is *restored* to the fold. In their original setting the parables of the lost sheep and of the prodigal son were a defense of Jesus' outreach to tax collectors and sinners excommunicated from the synagogue. Today people usually apply these parables to the missionary or evangelistic situation and thus take them to reflect someone's initial salvation. However, in the context of Jesus' teaching these parables reflected the restoration of excommunicated people.

Too often the church has cajoled and even coerced confessions, rather than eliciting them as a joyful rediscovery of the Christian way. Furthermore, such confessions frequently seem to be an embarrassment for the congregation rather than a celebration. These marks betray a departure from the good news of the gospel as a basis for discipline. Where church discipline functions on the basis of the gospel, there confession is always a celebration of grace, because it is ultimately a confession of faith.

We have now seen the nature of confession in the context of church discipline. If an individual has sinned, the confession which an evangelical admonition expects will include an honest acknowledgment of failure. If someone has really seen the joy of the Christian way as a live option, he or she will no longer attempt any evasion or denial. This acknowledgment of sin is never an end in itself, however, but only an avenue to the confession of faith. Confession of sin has the valuable function of enabling a sinner to make a deliberate repudiation of sin for the way of Christ. The recovery of a genuine Christian spirit and conduct is evidence that a given confession of sin has fulfilled this function.

Some people such as those in Alcoholics Anonymous have discovered an important and essential element in the confession of sin. Confession is the end of denial and the beginning of the admission of the truth about oneself. Without this there is no potential to move forward into a new life. Facing reality is a prerequisite to the ability to overcome sin and the capacity to leave it behind.

At the same time, there is a danger of some confessions of sin indulging in exhibitionism. Some offenders never stop baring their souls, like those "true confessions" books or celebrity converts that seem to invite their hearers or readers to "play the voyeur."[6] As already noted, confession is an act, a step into a new life, not a state of mind at which to get stalled.

A church involved in discipline would therefore do well to look at the spirit and fruit of a confession rather than at the quantity of details dredged up. The test of a sincere confession is not just the factual accuracy of a report of someone's past behavior. It is the evidence of a new lifestyle which shows that the person is leaving such behavior behind. The church's goal in all of this is the recovery of healthy Christian life. And that by its very nature is joyfully confessed, publicly and openly.

In principle, then, all confession should wish to be public, in discipline as in conversion. Something is wrong with a convert who seeks to hide her faith. Matthew 18 implies that one may decide whether confession will be public or private largely by the stage at which an individual responds to admonition. The church of the first few centuries consistently required persons under discipline to make a public confession. Scholars do not agree whether this confession involved a public recitation of sins or only public acts of penance. Clearly, however, the formal acts of penitence (wearing sackcloth, fasting, giving alms, and going through prescribed stages of restoration) were almost invariably public. The restoration or readmission of penitents in an Easter congregational service was also public. (This Easter connection, by the way, further suggests its parallel to the baptism of converts at that season.) Auricular confession in the later medieval Catholic Church was, of course, invariably private.

In the first centuries, the confession and the restoration which followed it were always cases involving excommunicated persons. We should not take for granted, therefore, that cases which do not go as far as excommunication will necessarily involve public confession. If someone under admonition heeds that admonition, the church is to forgive that person privately. The matter does not require a public confession.

Only if the person refuses to heed the private admonition is the matter brought before the church, because the question then becomes one of membership itself. Since this affects the entire congregation, it calls for their awareness. If an individual responds to disciplinary counsel at this last level, it will in the nature of the case be a public confession.

In Matthew's prescription for dealing with an erring believer, going to the whole church is a last resort. This implies the possibility if not the likelihood of a positive response early in the process. In those instances church discipline might well involve only private confession and forgiveness.

There may, of course, be other considerations in a particular case that would suggest public confession. In general, a confession should be as public as the sin was. If a person's lapse is known publicly, the church may deem it appropriate for the confession also to be public.[7] But public confession should not be seen as a punishment or a deterrent to sin.

The process of admonition, repentance, and forgiveness is a kind of dialogue. Admonition invites the response of repentance, which in turn calls for the reply of forgiveness. Like repentance, forgiveness too is an act. It is the joyful acknowledgment of repentance and the reinforcement of the turnaround it signifies.

Forgiveness is the realization of the discipled life. In discipline, as in evangelism, the church seeks nothing more and settles for nothing less. Forgiveness and righteousness are achieved where someone responds to admonition. The goal of discipline is thus a return to the normal, healthy, sanctified life of the whole community of faith.

There may be times when the church legitimately declines to forgive, and not because of hardheartedness or a mean spirit. The church should always be *willing* to forgive. That, in fact, is what the word of admonition implies. However, the formal act of forgiveness should occur only where the church recognizes penitence and the abandonment of sin.

As the church declines to baptize those who are not turning to righteousness in deed and in truth, so the church must decline to grant absolution where there is not true repentance and amendment of life. Accepting responsibility for the discernment needed to forgive with integrity is essential to the church's ministry of watch and care over erring members.

When admonition meets only persistent impenitence, the church must eventually speak the word of excommunication, as we will see in the following chapter.

5

REDEMPTIVE EXCOMMUNICATION
"Gentile and Tax Collector"

Excommunication does not represent a breakdown of grace or a departure from the gospel. Excommunication is the form under which the church continues to extend the gospel to the impenitent.

What should the church do with people who do not respond in repentance to the repeated word of admonition? According to Matthew 18:17, failure to hear the word of admonition calls for further action. "If he refuses to listen even to the church, let him be to you as a Gentile and a tax collector."

Many interpreters take this word of Jesus to mean excommunication. In the eyes of Judaism the Gentile was, of course, someone outside the community of faith. The tax collector signified someone who by compromise with the Roman occupation of the land had apostatized from the community of Israel and was therefore banned. Hence the presumptive meaning of the text seems to be exclusion from the church.

Withholding Communion

Historically, one of the persistent problems in church discipline has been the relationship between excommunication and communion. Sometimes suspension from communion has been a first step on the way to full excommunication. Sometimes the church has considered it the full equivalent of excommunication, since communion is for many churches the central symbol of membership and participation in the body of Christ.

There are two opposite inclinations on this issue. On the one hand, some people advocate leaving the Lord's Supper open to those who have sinned and are under discipline. They may even make a special effort to have them participate. The rationale for this is that the Lord's Supper is the means of grace, and who needs this more than the impenitent sinner? Continued access to the means of grace, it is alleged, may bring the sinner to repentance.

On the other hand, some advocate withholding communion from those under discipline. They are afraid that such participation would desecrate the Lord's table, harm the witness of the church, and bring damnation on the sinner because of unworthy participation (1 Cor. 11:27-32).

An answer to this apparent dilemma must begin with a proper understanding of the meaning of the Lord's Supper. The Lord's Supper is a confessional act in which people who present themselves at the Lord's table declare to each other and to the world that they stand in covenant relationship with God. By participating they also declare that they accept the consequences of this covenant—namely, forgiveness and fellowship. Thus it is appropriate that all who have covenanted discipleship should participate in the enacted confession of this covenant. Conversely, all who participate in the Lord's Supper should manifest the life of discipleship which participation professes.

Therefore, participation in the Lord's Supper on the part of impenitent sinners is a serious contradiction, since participation in communion is inconsistent with their life. Such persons are living a lie. They may try to deceive themselves about it—and others too—but sooner or later the hypocrisy will exact its judgment. It is a fundamental law of life that people who indulge in self-deception eventually destroy themselves.

In the light of this, and to prevent a person from "eating and drinking judgment upon himself," many believe the proper course is to withhold communion. A little reflection will show, however, that this has an undesirable implication. For if participation in communion is a repeated act of confession of faith, then suspending someone from communion is in effect to pronounce that person to be without faith. That is, banning someone from the Lord's table implies excommunication from the community of faith.

Usually, however, the church does not intend to signify full excommunication by suspension from communion. Instead, the church intends to signify that a given person is not in fact the faithful disciple that participation in communion would profess. At the same time it makes room for continued communionless membership in the church, implying the possibility of a second level of membership on a basis other than responsive discipleship.

To tolerate impenitent church members, even if denied communion, merely repeats in slightly different form the misunderstanding of the other policy of condoning impenitent participation in communion. Where lenience makes room for faithful and faithless communing membership, strict suspension makes room for faithful communing and faithless noncommuning membership. Both arrangements suggest two kinds of membership, two levels of existence in the church—penitent and impenitent, forgiven and unforgiven.

This surely is not an acceptable system. Where can we look for a better one? I would suggest that we look to the examples of Jesus at the Last Supper and of Paul in 1 Corinthians 5.

Judas at the Last Supper

Some writers on church discipline like to claim that Jesus tolerated Judas among his disciples at the Last Supper despite his knowledge that Judas was a hypocrite, had defected, and would betray him. From this they conclude that the church too must tolerate hypocrites and sinners within its membership.

Some writers debate whether Judas did or did not receive the bread and the cup at the Supper. However, whether or not food entered his digestive system is irrelevant. The crucial thing was the challenge to faithful discipleship that met Judas in the bread and the cup and the decision he made in response to it. Jesus' act of offering him the sop was an invitation to him to change his mind and remain a member of the disciple community—a most awesome admonition. Judas could have made the decision to heed this admonition by eating in good faith and changing his mind about the betrayal he had planned. But he rejected the invitation, as shown by his departure. By this decision he effectively removed himself from the community.

There is no truth, then, to the claim that Jesus tolerated a hypocrite among his disciples. But neither did Jesus begin by excluding him from the Supper. Jesus began with an encouragement to Judas to participate, conveying the understanding that participation with integrity called for a radical about-face in thought and deed. Jesus structured the situation to combine loving concern with the demand for an honest decision. The Last Supper was thus the setting for an attempt at rediscipling a hypocrite. It ended, alas, with a negative decision.

This example may thus show how discipline can actually take place *in the context of* communion, for communion itself becomes the invitation to continued discipleship. Rightly conducted, communion becomes the setting in which persons by the nature of their response can be constrained to come to a decision.

Paul in 1 Corinthians 5 followed a procedure that at first sight seems the opposite of what Jesus did at the Last Supper. Where Jesus offered Judas continued communion, Paul called the church to withhold communion—"not even to eat with such a one" (1 Cor. 5:11). Between the two situations there is an underlying difference, however. The case in Corinth involved a man who presented himself repeatedly at the Lord's table while refusing to quit an immoral life. Since he himself was unable or unwilling to resolve this self-contradiction, the church had to step in. It had to declare to him that it could not be partner to his hypocrisy by continued communion with him. The church informed him of his condition through excommunication.

It is not hard to see the fundamental difference between the biblical principles we have sketched here and the practice of the church in much of its history. In discipline according to the gospel, the church should not arbitrarily begin with suspension from communion but with a fervent invitation to repentance. If this invitation goes unheeded, the church out of love does not, however, permit individuals to destroy themselves unwarned. The church then resorts to excommunication to safeguard the meaning of that gospel by which alone people can be liberated from the power of sin.[1]

The tradition of communing and noncommuning levels of membership in the church is neither biblical nor wise. Normative Christianity should mean communing membership. Otherwise, there will be a recurrent inclination to think some people are not "good enough" for communion. Church members may, in fact, think this about themselves.

People who are "good enough" for membership are, in fact, good enough for communion. People who are not "good enough" for communion are not good enough for membership in the church. For if there is some obstacle to eating together, it is a sign that there is something wrong that needs to be made right. Coming together to eat is an opportune occasion to make relationships right. This assumes, of course, a Lord's Supper at which real communication takes place. This may call for returning to an agape feast at which the church engages in serious spiritual business.

In some cases of church discipline the issue of communion may not arise, especially if the church celebrates communion infrequently enough to settle problems between communion seasons. But if a problem does arise, the church must beware of either judging too hastily or condoning hypocritical participation. In either case the church hurts itself, the individual, and the cause of the gospel in the world.

As already noted, church membership includes participation in communion. We must remember that persons under admonition are still members of the church. Only if they refuse to heed the admonition of the church are they excommunicated—that is, simply and completely excluded from membership in the body of Christ. As "Gentile and tax collector" they are then once more the object of Christ's call to discipleship.

Major and Minor Excommunication

For a long stretch of its history the church has distinguished major and minor excommunication, or the greater and lesser ban. Sometimes the church added the anathema as a third and most severe degree of excommunication, though usually the church regarded it as an aggravated major excommunication. A Catholic writer states "that in former times the ancient Christians knew nothing of the system of major excommunication."[2] According to an old Catholic encyclopedia, since 1884 the Catholic Church holds to only major excommunication.[3]

What can one say to this question? The discussion above rejected the idea of two levels of membership in the church, faithful membership with communion and faithless membership without it. It is even more absurd to propose two levels or degrees of nonmembership. We may speak facetiously of half-converted people, but we cannot seriously entertain the notion of half-baptized persons who are halfway into the membership of the church! Why then half-excommunication? Although the church must allow a person time to struggle toward a decision, the gospel finally postulates only two positions, faith and unbelief.

The medieval notion of major and minor excommunication

arose through a confusion of church and state. Since everyone was a member of the church, excommunication necessarily entailed the suspension of religious privileges. Since Christianity was the officially established state religion, excommunication logically entailed also the suspension of people's civil rights, including such things as citizenship, guild membership, legal rights, and economic rights.[4] Anyone who understands the gospel will not propose that we return to that.

Even today there are many ways, some of them quite subtle, in which members of the church can inflict punishment upon those under church discipline. Fortunately, we do have a separation of church and state in the United States and Canada. People in our churches may not even know medieval terms such as major excommunication. Nevertheless, it is possible to ostracize persons socially, boycott their business, or in some way discriminate against them. This resort to punitive measures cannot achieve redemptive restoration to the Christian way.

Destruction of the Flesh

In connection with the subject of excommunication there frequently arises the question of the meaning of an expression appearing twice in the New Testament. It appears in 1 Corinthians 5:5 and in 1 Timothy 1:20: "delivered to Satan." First Corinthians adds the phrase "for the destruction of the flesh."

Many interpreters argue that delivering someone "to Satan for the destruction of the flesh" suggests more than just treating someone as a Gentile and a tax collector.

This invites the question whether Paul's counsel in 1 Corinthians 5:5 and the instructions in 1 Timothy 1:20 conflict with the instructions of Jesus. The action described by Paul seems to imply the infliction of punishment, not merely the passive surrender of an impenitent person. These writers take "destruction of the flesh" to mean consignment to physical suffering, perhaps even death. Some have suggested that Paul was resorting to a technique used by people in the pagan religions of the time.

> A person who had been wronged by another and had no other way of retaliating, consigned the criminal to the god, and left the punishment to be inflicted by divine power. In the invocations, the god was asked or expected to punish the wrongdoer by bodily disease; thus any bodily affliction which came on the accused person was regarded, by both the invoker and the sufferer, as the messenger or weapon of the god.[5]

There is certainly no reason for reading such ideas of vindictiveness into Paul. The act of handing an individual over to Satan was precisely a refusal to retaliate, a determination to leave judgment to God.

Some writers, noting the words, "That his spirit may be saved in the day of the Lord Jesus," suggest that Paul is employing a doctrine of purgatory. They cite 1 Corinthians 3:13 and 11:32 as further evidence of Paul's belief that sin may be expiated by temporal suffering. Elect souls who endure it will thereby be saved at the last day.

The suggestion of a connection between sin and sickness is not unthinkable. There is a hint of such a connection in both the story of the healing of the paralytic (Matt. 9:2-5) and in James 5:13-18. Now forgiveness may indeed lead to healing, and unforgiven sin may indeed lead to sickness and suffering. However, such sickness, suffering, and even death do not necessarily lead to forgiveness.

It is not necessary to look for complicated explanations of Paul's thought and action on this subject. The idea of a "destruction of the flesh" has for its background the experience of regeneration and baptism. In Romans 6:6, for example, Paul says, "We know that our old self was crucified with . . . [Christ] so that the sinful body might be destroyed." In Colossians 3:5 he says, "Put to death therefore what is earthly in you."

Surely we are not to understand these texts to mean the infliction of physical suffering! Nor is it necessary to read it into 1 Corinthians 5:5.[6] As one commentator explains, "destruction of the flesh" means "the annihilation of the demonic powers and the sinful self that has handed itself over to them." Flesh signifies "everything in us which is in thrall to the power of sin because of our passionate propensities."[7]

"Destruction of the flesh" and "salvation of the spirit" are correlatives. "Destruction of the flesh" was to have been realized already at the conversion and baptism of the immoral person referred to in 1 Corinthians 5:5. His lapse from grace, therefore, obliged the church to make the new offer of grace through the shock treatment of excommunication. The hope was that this might achieve that destruction of the sinful self and the salvation of the spirit which had somehow not yet been realized.

This does not suggest that the sin and rejection of grace for which the church excommunicates someone will not lead to suffering. Nor does it suggest that God might not use such suffering for good purposes. As noted above, not to submit to the reign of God in Christ is to put oneself under the rule of Satan and sin. "For the wages of sin is death" (Rom. 3:23). However, in the body of Christ the Spirit delivers people from the power of death and gives them life (Rom. 7:24; 8:2).

The phrase *destruction of the flesh* in 1 Corinthians 5:5 does not justify an excommunication intended to inflict physical suffering. As one author says, deliverance to Satan "is neither the imposition of a civil penalty nor the infliction of bodily pain." Rather, it is "simply expulsion from the Christian society."[8] This is also how the early Puritans understood it in a congregational confession of 1589.[9]

Deliverance to Satan does not imply a severe form of excommunication. It is absurd to suggest that Paul failed to follow the example of the gentle and loving Jesus. *The Interpreter's Bible* asks, "Was Paul insisting upon a wise course of action? Would Jesus have done this, or would he have been more merciful toward the sinful?" This invites the rejoinder that Jesus did do precisely what Paul here advises and is likely Paul's example. Jesus' dealing with Judas is nothing other than a deliverance to Satan, even if it did not apparently achieve his salvation.

Most scholars interpret Paul's expression somehow or other to mean simply excommunication. A representative biblical commentator states:

> Delivering to Satan apparently signifies excommunication (see verses 2, 7, 13). The idea underlying this is that outside the church is the sphere of Satan (Eph. 2:12; Col. 1:13; 1 John 5:19). To be expelled from the Church of Christ is to be delivered over into that region where Satan holds sway.[10]

One writer on church discipline, commenting on 1 Timothy 1:20, says that handing people over to Satan means "to put them for a time outside the communion of the church . . . into the realm of the princes of this world of darkness so that, deprived of the special grace of the community, . . . they may realize the consequence of the error of their ways."[11]

First Corinthians 5:5 is not, then, a case of a serious form of excommunication. Rather, it shows how serious excommunication is. It is better to use this passage in formulating an overall understanding of excommunication than to bring to it a preconceived notion of excommunication in order to find here an aberration. Paul teaches us that excommunication is serious business.

Anathema

The connection of an *anathema* with excommunication is not as clear in the New Testament as is the connection of the phrase *delivered to Satan. Anathema* became associated with excommunication in the Middle Ages. According to one authority, "During the first centuries the anathema did not seem to differ from the sentence of excommunication [but] beginning with the sixth century a distinction was made between the two." Excommunication signified separation "from the society of the brethren," and anathema separation "from the body of Christ, which is the church." Thus the anathema came to be defined as an especially solemn excommunication.[12]

When Pope Zachary (731-752) drew up the formulation for the anathema, he distinguished three sorts of excommunication: minor, major, and anathema. The anathema was "the penalty incurred by crimes of the gravest order, and solemnly promulgated by the Pope."[13] However, an anathematized person could still repent and be absolved.

Calvin followed the medieval church in distinguishing excommunication from anathema. However, he differed with the medieval church in claiming that the anathema, "completely excluding pardon, dooms and devotes the individual to eternal destruction." The anathema, he added, fortunately, "is rarely if ever to be used." Calvin did use it on Michael Servetus, however, burning him at the stake.[14] Thus, for Calvin, the anathema was actually the death penalty.

Although its connection with discipline is quite tenuous in the few New Testament texts mentioning it (Rom. 9:3; 1 Cor. 12:3; 16:22; Gal. 1:8-9), the anathema has a meaning in biblical thought that is not inconsistent with the gospel. The Old Testament speaks of a curse, often used on enemies of Israel, that could also fall on a member of Israel such as Achan. This curse was the penalty of death, and it therefore removed Achan from the community (Josh. 7).

Later in the evolution of the practice of discipline in Judaism the curse no longer imposed the death penalty. A symbolic funeral ceremony replaced execution. This ceremony symbolized the spiritual death of an Israelite in being cut off from the people of God through the curse of an excommunication. Strict Judaism treated an excommunicated person as dead, cut off from the living community of Israel.

In the New Testament Paul uses this language from his

Jewish heritage when he says, "If any one has no love for the Lord, let him be accursed" (1 Cor. 16:22)." We concur with the commentator who remarks: "The world was divided into two classes, those who loved, with however many failings and backslidings, the Lord Jesus, and those who hated him. It is the latter who are anathematized."[15] That is, the church commits them to the realm lying under the curse.

Between the garden of Eden, where the curse descends, and the eschatological garden of paradise, where it is lifted, the world lies under the curse. But Christ bore away the curse, and his deliverance becomes effective for those believing in him. Those, however, who do not love Christ still stand under the curse.

This term from another age and culture sounds strange to modern ears. Paul's simple twofold classification in 1 Corinthians 16:22 shows, however, that anathema is simply synonymous with excommunication. There is no justification for introducing punitive and legalistic connotations from outside the gospel.

With this background we can now examine the significance of the Ananias and Sapphira story of Acts 5. People often recall this story in connection with church discipline because they correctly consider it to be a case of anathema. There is a clear parallel between this story and that of Achan in Joshua 7. In each case the sin of greed invades the pristine community. In each case there is a supernatural disclosure of guilt. And in each case the culprit is removed from the community by a divinely sanctioned sudden death.

Might this story justify the church in ever using the death penalty in discipline? Jean Lasserre finds it surprising that John Calvin sees in Acts 5 justification for the occasional use of capital punishment by the church.

When it comes to the gospel miracles, says Lasserre, Calvin thinks we have a phenomenon restricted to the primitive era of the church.

But astonishingly enough [Calvin] never asks himself whether the miraculous punishments too may be strictly confined to this period. . . . It cannot be admitted that they are part of an ecclesiastical discipline for which they would be normative models.

But, asks Lasserre, since Calvin insisted on finding guidance for discipline in Acts 5, "Did he himself ever administer physical punishment to an adversary by the power of his words alone?" Acts 5 does not justify "the capital executions of which the church, alas, has carried out too many, with or without the aid of the secular arm."[16] Nor does it justify a resort to punitive notions inconsistent with the gospel. God has the right to intervene and take life at any time, early or late. And God has the right to use so-called natural or supernatural means, even if that cuts off for some individuals the day of opportunity for repentance.

The point, however, is exactly that the imposition of death is a divine prerogative. Hence it is not necessary to posit instances in which the church pronounces an excommunication of such gravity that it carries the sentence of death. Peter called Ananias and Sapphira to account, but there is not even the hint of a sword, gallows, firing squad, electric chair, or lethal injection as one of the possible instruments of church discipline.

Nor is it necessary to posit certain forms of excommunication that preclude the possibility of repentance. Even the Jewish curse left room for repentance, as did the medieval church's anathema. The Ananias and Sapphira story symbolizes the spiritual death entailed in excommunication. Theirs is a case of mortal sin, to put it in early and medieval church terms. It stands in the story of the apostolic church as a warning to the Christian community as the story of Achan did to Israel.

Is Excommunication Christian?

Some writers question whether the New Testament supports the practice of excommunication. They even question that the primitive church practiced it. The prevailing tone of the New Testament message, they say, is forgiving love. An act of judgment such as excommunication would contradict this. Thus one scholar says:

> A painstaking exegesis makes clear that the church did not know of a formal excommunication. The case of the deliverance to Satan (1 Cor. 5) has to do with a direct intervention of the Lord. In all other cases it is the church or congregation that withdraws, separates itself, and suspends table fellowship. And that is not the same thing as excommunication. These nuances are not incidental.[17]

Several writers on discipline share this concern. They believe the term *excommunication* has picked up connotations from the history of Christianity—things such as coercion and civil punishments that are inconsistent with the teaching of the New Testament.

Excommunication is not, of course, a biblical word, but then neither is its root, *communion*, or fellowship. Unless we are ready to abandon the term *communion* as well, the issue is whether we will define excommunication according to the message and spirit of the New Testament or according to un-evangelical practices in the history of Christianity. That issue remains even if we switch to other terms for excommunication, such as *disfellowshiping* or *dropping people from membership.*

It is undeniable that Matthew 18:17 and other New Testament texts envisage an act that can be called excommunication.

> When unfaithful members of the church plainly declare by their actions that they choose rather to obey the laws of Satan than the commands of Christ, . . . when men have by their own choice and by the actions of their life in effect placed themselves outside her communion, the church solemnly refuses to receive them back until they repent and testify their desire to be restored again to a state of salvation.[18]

If we should not call excommunication a formal act, it is logical to infer that baptism and receiving someone into the body of Christ also should not be recognized as a formal act. For excommunication, like baptism, is an official church act concerning membership.

Yet we do not object to considering baptism a formal act. Excommunication is, in effect, the reverse of baptism. It officially ends someone's church membership in the way baptism officially begins it. We must therefore also recognize the formal act of excommunication, because baptism and excommunication are correlatives.

The church is also tempted to run away from the responsibility of excommunication because it is a painful task. Those who propose to do away with formal excommunication may intend to excuse the church from the responsibility of dealing with continued impenitence in its membership.

Unfortunately, there has been bad excommunication practice. This has conditioned the thinking of many people to the point where they can see nothing redemptive in the dismissal of a member from the church. Therefore it is essential to see that *excommunication does not represent a breakdown of grace or a departure from the gospel.* Excommunication is a renewed presentation of the gospel message to impenitent persons in that it confronts them with the truth. As Paul says in 1 Corinthians 6:9, "The unrighteous will not inherit the kingdom of God."

To utter this truth in warning to those who have abandoned the obedience of faith is as consistent with the nature of the gospel as informing people in evangelism that unless they repent and believe the gospel they cannot enter the kingdom of God (John 3:5). Thus excommunication, rightly practiced, never cuts people off from grace. On the contrary, its function is to prevent persons from anesthetizing themselves against grace. *Excommunication is the form under which the church continues to extend the gospel to the impenitent.*

Excommunication is not, then, loveless condemnation. It does not represent a failure of church discipline. It is as necessary in spiritual life as candid diagnosis is in medical practice. Persons cannot find spiritual healing without facing the truth. Far from being unloving, evangelical excommunication is the only loving and redeeming course of action possible toward impenitent individuals in given circumstances. It is also the only appropriate way for the church to preserve its integrity and its witness to the world.

Excommunication should always, of course, include the invitation to restoration.

6

AVOIDANCE AND RESTORATION
"Warn Him as a Brother"

Jesus' attitude toward "tax collectors and sinners"
in the Gospels is the model of Christian avoidance.

The subject of excommunication sooner or later raises the question of avoidance, often called "shunning." The question is logical because avoidance has to do with the treatment of someone who has been excommunicated.

The Biblical Basis
Many people see avoidance or shunning as an eccentricity of narrow-minded religious sects. More careful investigation shows that some form of avoidance has a firm base in the New Testament. The counsel in Matthew 18:17 to treat an impenitent individual as a Gentile or a tax collector implies it. Several other New Testament texts explicitly teach avoidance. They are important enough to cite here.

> Take note of those who create dissensions and difficulties, in opposition to the doctrine which you have been taught; avoid them. (Rom. 16:17)

> I wrote to you not to associate with any one who bears the name of brother if he is guilty of immorality or greed, or is an

idolater, reviler, drunkard, or robber—not even to eat with such a one. (1 Cor. 5:11)

Keep away from any brother who is living in idleness and not in accord with the tradition that you received from us. . . . If any one refuses to obey what we say in this letter, note that man, and have nothing to do with him, that he may be ashamed. Do not look on him as an enemy, but warn him as a brother. (2 Thess. 3:6, 14-15)

For [in the last days] men will be lovers of self . . . lovers of pleasure rather than lovers of God, holding the form of religion but denying the power of it. Avoid such people. (2 Tim. 3:2-5)

As for a man who is factious, after admonishing him once or twice, have nothing more to do with him. (Titus 3:10)

This is a forceful array of texts from five different books of the New Testament—six, if we include Matthew. They show that one cannot write off avoidance as a custom of sectarians. It must be reexamined and understood within the framework of a truly Christian church discipline.

Ostracism Within the Church?

One form of avoidance is ostracism before full excommunication. Second Thessalonians 3:14-15 ("Do not look on him as an enemy, but warn him as a brother") especially lends itself to this view. Thus one writer says on this text:

There is no necessary suggestion of excommunication. Probably some kind of separation is implied. It is not that the man is to be separated from the church, but rather that the church is to avoid the man. It seems at least reasonable to infer that . . . the offender might while still enjoying such privileges as he cared to avail himself of, be treated with a certain coldness, ostracized socially if not yet ecclesiastically. Or an act of discipline may be implied, the man being refused communion for a space. But no definite conclusion can be reached from such vague premises.[1]

A Puritan congregational conference of 1589 took this same view. It interpreted 2 Thessalonians 3:15 to mean "sharply reprehend" and "gravely admonish" an offender before excommunicating him, "prooving if at any time the Lord will give him repentaunce." Puritans were also to avoid someone fully excommunicated. This served as a warning to the congregation "to abstaine themselves from his societie."[2]

One modern theologian tries to make the same point about a "withdrawal" before full exclusion. This withdrawal includes excommunication, defined as expulsion from the Lord's Supper, which, he avers, "is the literal meaning of the word." Already at the time the case comes before the whole congregation, the church must distinguish this withdrawal carefully from full exclusion. "Removal from the midst" is this theologian's translation of Paul's term in 1 Corinthians 5:2.[3]

Now, one can insist on defining the verb *excommunicate* according to one old meaning of the term *communicate*—"to receive communion" (*Webster's*). However, the common use of the term *excommunication* is "to cast out of the communion of the church" (*Webster's*), to "exclude from religious membership" (*American Heritage*).

The distinction between two kinds of avoidance cannot find justification in 1 Corinthians 5, the very passage to which people appeal. For there "removal from the midst" (5:2) and "not even to eat with such a one" refer to the same case, a fully excluded person. They therefore define the same relationship. Paul's 1 Corinthians 5:6-8 passage contains several allusions to the Lord's Supper implications of an excommunication:

•Cleanse out the old leaven.
•Christ, our paschal lamb, has been sacrificed.
•Let us . . . celebrate the festival, not with the old leaven . . . of malice and evil.

These allusions all have to do with circumspect conduct toward the fully excluded individual. We cannot with integrity read back into 1 Corinthians 5 the modern practice of withholding communion from church members.

Second Thessalonians 3:14-15 seems to be the main basis for the notion of avoidance before full exclusion. Does *brother* describe the attitude desired in the admonishers, or does it indicate the status of the person being admonished? No one can answer conclusively on the basis of the grammar alone. However, the word for avoidance here (*sunanamignusthai*) occurs only three times in the New Testament. It is the same as that employed twice in 1 Corinthians 5:9, 11, the text just discussed. There the context unambiguously establishes its meaning as full excommunication. (Read 1 Cor. 5:3-5.) Second Thessalonians 3:14-15 says nothing about the Lord's Supper.

The notion of an ostracism before exclusion from the church comes from church tradition. It has neither a biblical base nor a logical one. According to the theology of discipling in this book, rejection of the gospel is the decisive ground for breaking fellowship. It is, in fact, the only thing that should be allowed to disrupt fellowship. For that reason seeing avoidance as an ostracism within the church is inconsistent with the nature of the church. As long as persons are Christian brothers or sisters, fellowship is normative and should continue, even if it includes the appeal for penitence. It is quite inconsistent to plead with believers to *remain* believers while avoiding them as if they had already become unbelievers.

Only when a person ceases to be a Christian brother or sister through persistent impenitence is this fellowship broken. Even then the very breaking of fellowship becomes a reminder that that person has ceased to be a brother or sister and begins the invitation to return. Recourse to an ostracism without complete excommunication moves once more in the direction of major and minor excommunications. This view we discussed in the previous chapter and found incompatible with the gospel.

Jesus and Tax Collectors

The central significance of avoidance is clear from Jesus' words about treating someone like a Gentile and tax collector. The way Jesus reached out to these ostracized people is a well-established point in the Gospels. *The tax collectors and sinners spoken of in the Gospels usually had been excommunicated from the Jewish community. Jesus' attitude toward them is thus the model of Christian avoidance.*

Five passages in the synoptic Gospels (exclusive of parallels) attest to this.

In Matthew 9:9-13 Jesus calls the tax collector Levi to be his disciple. Jesus eats with tax collectors, causing the Pharisees to ask, "Why does your teacher eat with tax collectors and sinners?"

In Matthew 11:19 Jesus quotes a criticism he has heard about himself, "Behold, a glutton and a drunkard, a friend of tax collectors and sinners!"

In Luke 15:1-10 the tax collectors and sinners reportedly approach Jesus. Again the Pharisees and scribes murmur, "This man receives sinners and eats with them." This prompts Jesus to tell the parables of the lost sheep and of the prodigal son.

In Luke 18:9-14 Jesus tells the story of two men going into the temple to pray, one a Pharisee and the other a tax collector. According to Jesus, only the tax collector, who said, "God, be merciful to me a sinner!" went down to his house justified.

In Luke 19:1-10 Zacchaeus is converted on the occasion of Jesus' visit to his house. "Today salvation has come to this house," says Jesus, "since he also is a son of Abraham. For the Son of man came to seek and to save the lost."

So Jesus' treatment of these outcasts was notorious and contrasted markedly with the usual conventions of the day. It became a prominent theme in the gospel tradition. Of course, we should not draw ridiculous conclusions from this. To hear some people tell it, Jesus habitually hobnobbed with such people, jovially and uncritically, but this is surely not the case.

For while he did not ostracize them or treat them as social untouchables, he did not pretend that they were okay. On the contrary, Jesus sought them out to "save" them, as Luke 19:10 (cited above) shows. He presumably considered them "lost" and in need of restoration. What is most important, his contact with them somehow transformed them and made new people out of them.

The clue to the meaning of Jesus' words about relating to excommunicated people is the conduct of Jesus himself. If this is true, then avoidance treats such persons as prime candidates for the call to discipleship. Of course, this also unambiguously implies that their present standing is outside the way of Christ.

Avoidance Is Communication

Avoidance is the adoption of an especially discreet relationship with excommunicated persons that brings home to them the truth about their spiritual condition. It does not permit them to escape into self-deception. It means refusing to pretend that persons are Christians after they have ceased to be such. It means respecting their decisions and honestly treating them as persons of the world. Like excommunication, it is a form of continuing to present the gospel.

Avoidance must say two things simultaneously, first, that a given person has forsaken the way of discipleship; and second, that he or she has a standing invitation to return to it.

Avoidance, then, is a process of communication and not, as some might infer from the word *excommunication,* cutting off communication. Nor is it a system of punishment, coercion, blacklisting, or ostracizing someone as a social outcast. Instead, it is the appropriate way of presenting the invitation to discipleship to someone who is leaving it.

Discretion is needed in this task. The church must not cut off communication. Nor can it afford to mix its signals, canceling the message of excommunication by the informal everyday attitude of its members toward excommunicated persons. A backslapping camaraderie can easily contradict what the church is saying by its formal excommunication. This inconsistency only confuses excommunicated people. It leads them to deceive themselves about their condition and to anesthetize themselves against the call of the gospel.

The purpose of avoidance is clear communication not only with the person involved but also with other Christians in the church and with non-Christians in the world. Some Christians by their conduct toward an excommunicated person do not acknowledge the practical implications of that excommunication. They thus unconsciously mislead their fellow Christians—and unbelievers as well. Their actions suggest to others that a lapse from the faith and its consequent excommunication do not really matter and do not affect a person's spiritual status.

Thus it encourages people on all sides to deceive themselves and each other into thinking that nothing serious is amiss. The consequences of this are understandably disastrous for the total cause of the Christian community. "One does not accomplish restoration ... where everything proceeds as if nothing had happened."[4]

Paul's teaching in 1 Corinthians 5:9 supports the interpretation of avoidance we are sketching here. When the apostle enjoins the Corinthian church not to eat with a persistent sinner, he is speaking primarily of the Lord's Supper. He is likely also counseling discontinuation of any associations which the excommunicated individual, other Christians, or the world might construe as continued or resumed Christian fellowship.

Paul immediately warns his readers against drawing absurd conclusions from his counsel on avoidance (see 1 Cor. 5:10). Elsewhere he goes on record as holding no objection to secular table fellowship (1 Cor. 10:27). Nevertheless, in the Corinthian correspondence he repeatedly warns Christians against relationships that would mislead fellow Christians, deceive themselves, or obscure the church's witness to the world.

Therefore, an effective and truly Christian practice of avoidance presupposes public excommunication—public in the sense of informing members of an affected congregation. The purpose is not, of course, public humiliation. Officials in a congregation may try to keep an excommunication secret to protect an individual or congregation from public embarrassment. But only confusion can result when the leaders keep church members ignorant of someone's removal from membership. Because of being uninformed, members will be totally unprepared to relate appropriately to that person. In this technical sense, excommunication must be public because it involves an altered relation between the excommunicated individual and every other member of the church. Such is simply the reality of responsible interpersonal relationships implied by church membership.

The point just made is in line with the recognition of the importance of congregational participation in baptism. For this also involves a new pattern of relationships between the new member and every other person in the congregation. Excommunication is, as noted earlier, the reverse of baptism. At baptism the whole church under its Lord acknowledges the act of faith and endorses Christ's incorporation of this individual into the church. It becomes Christ's agent in the incorporation and accepts in life the implications of that fact. In an excommunication the whole church acknowledges the person's unfaith, endorses Christ's exclusion, becomes the agency of that exclusion, and accepts the practical implications of that fact.

Marital Avoidance

An understanding of the meaning of avoidance provides a background for examining the special type of avoidance called marital shunning. Some denominations have made avoidance signify a rather severe, formal ostracism following excommunication. This avoidance, they have held, reaches even into the natural relationships of marriage and family.

Menno Simons held that "the rule for the ban is a general

rule, and excepts no one; neither husband nor wife, nor parent nor child."[5] Alexander Mack, founder of the Church of the Brethren, also supported the practice of avoidance, citing Deuteronomy 13:6-9. According to this passage, members of an idolater's own family should be the first to raise their hands against him to stone him. He also appealed to Matthew 10:37, which warns, "He who loves father or mother more than me is not worthy of me." However, like Menno Simons, Mack allowed members to contact excommunicated persons in order to admonish them to repent and to help them in physical want.[6]

Does the avoidance commanded by the biblical texts intend marital avoidance? Does avoidance extend to "bed and board"?

Now Jesus claimed that spiritual relationships sometimes cut directly across the natural relationships of life. "For I have come to set a man against his father, and a daughter against her mother ... and a man's foes will be those of his own household" (Matt. 10:35-36). People usually apply this to what may happen through conversions, but it may also apply to the result of an excommunication. Thus an individual may need to recognize that a given excommunication places a parent, spouse, or child outside the church.

This recognition that spiritual relationships may cut across natural ones reminds us that we are not to confuse these. Rigid shunning or marital avoidance does confuse these, since a break in spiritual fellowship between family members is thought to demand a break in natural social relationships.

Concerning marital avoidance, we should read 1 Corinthians 7:12-16, since it deals with the same problem in the context of conversion. Some conscientious new believers in Corinth thought the spiritual gulf their conversion had created between them and their unbelieving spouses called for a break in the natural relationship of marriage. Not so, replied the apostle Paul. When a married person becomes a Christian but the spouse does not, he or she should not seek to get divorced. In fact, the continuing natural association is *the occasion for* the life of witness to the unbelieving spouse. Peter's epistle makes the same point (1 Pet. 3:1-2).

Similarly in excommunication a break in spiritual relationships does not call for the dissolution of the marriage, a *de facto* divorce. Rather, the marriage becomes a setting for the opportunity of directing an individual back to the faith. True avoidance, then, is not disuse but discreet use of natural associations and relationships for this spiritual purpose.

Avoidance is only a continued reminder of what excommunication itself already declares. It is a sensitive and tactful use of social relationships to confront an individual with the meaning of the gospel. Although the biblical passages on avoidance do not specifically name excommunication, the absence of that term does not mean the principle is not involved.

Restoration

Restoration is the readmission to fellowship of an individual whom the church has been constrained to excommunicate. When Matthew speaks about treating someone like a Gentile and tax collector, he may be recalling how he was treated as a tax collector himself. For Matthew was once a candidate for the call to discipleship.

Now and then in the history of the church someone has suggested that excommunication is an irrevocable condemnation. However, being a form of presenting the gospel, excommunication implies by its very nature the opportunity for restoration. Although Matthew 18:15-20 does not refer to such a restoration, the preceding verses (18:10-14) speak of the return of the lost sheep. In the Jewish community the doors were open to restoration of even a person who had fallen under the great ban and was considered as dead.

Furthermore, Paul's instruction in 2 Corinthians 2:5-11 is to restore an individual with whom church discipline has achieved its purpose. (Whether this is the person mentioned in 1 Corinthians 5 is beside the point.) A restoration is envisaged also in 1 Timothy 1:20. Unless *may learn not to blaspheme* in this passage is merely vindictive, *learn* can only mean coming to the obedience of faith under the instruction of discipline.

In the postapostolic age of the church there were those who allowed no room for repentance and restoration of excommunicated persons. It was not long, however, before the Catholic Church readmitted penitents who had been guilty of even so-called mortal sins—at least on their deathbed. Even then, for some centuries the church permitted only one such restoration.

What is of interest here is the restoration procedure of the church during this era of public penance. In contrast to the New Testament, which says little about penitential procedure, the early Catholic Church prescribed an elaborate ritual of penance. In the penance of this era there were three or four stations of penance through which excommunicated penitents passed. However, the duration of the penance varied in different penitential books at different periods of this era.

Noteworthy in the early church's penitential system is the suggestion that genuine repentance was practically incidental. There were seeming exceptions to the rule, as in the statement that "The disposition and temper of the party under discipline are of principal account."[7] Thus one canonical epistle prescribes for murder nine years at each of three stations. If there is true repentance, the second and third stages may be reduced to eight, seven, or even five years.[8] In Basil's penitential the penance for a woman guilty of abortion is ten years. He says, however, "Let their treatment depend not on mere lapse of time, but on the character of their repentance."[9]

Several questions persistently arise in the face of this. Why was an individual, if truly penitent, required to serve time at all? Or, why should an individual even repent at all if time itself brought reinstatement and "true repentance" merely *reduced* the time?

Later centuries saw the order reversed. In earlier times penance preceded absolution. In later times penance followed absolution. If the sinner was paying for his sins, why not do it on credit? The reversed order and the fact that penance did not usually incur excommunication in these later centuries shows that repentance had lost its importance.

Both the early practice of disallowing restoration and the later system of restoration through penance reveal that the qualification for membership in the church was no longer the discipled life. First permanent excommunication, then in later history routine restoration—both without real regard to the erring member's spiritual attitude—showed that the church had moved away from repentance and faith as the basis of discipline.

One early church insight might have spared it this departure from the gospel into legalism, had the church followed the implications of that insight. Where it did permit a restoration of the excommunicated, the church of this era regarded the restoration as similar to baptism. Thus, penitents were classed and seated with catechumens and were absolved at the Easter baptismal season. This parallel between restoration and baptism shows the true conditions of restoration. They are, as in baptism, simply the authentic marks of spiritual life.

The church of this era went wrong in demanding secondary works of penance for restoration. One writer perceptively notes that the church never laid penitential requirements upon new converts, either in the New Testament or in the history of the church.[10] So if the church applies different requirements in restoration than it does in baptism, we can be sure that either baptism or restoration is misunderstood. Maybe both.

The perennial temptation of the church is to demand more for restoration than for baptism, to make the conditions for restoration more rigorous than for joining the body of Christ originally. The church is afraid the Lord might be too lenient or that he needs protection from those who might take advantage of his grace by sinning again.

According to Matthew 18:21-22 this problem occurred to Peter. So he asked, "How often shall my brother sin against me and I forgive him?" Christ then instructs Peter not to set any limits on divine grace. God himself is the guardian of grace and is quite able to protect himself against human hypocrisy. Where he grants persons repentance and the gift of faith, there the church must be ready to minister forgiveness. To add other conditions for restoration beyond a genuine return to the way of discipleship only hurts the cause, because it moves the church from its foundation in the gospel.

At times in its history the church has been plainly punitive in its restoration procedure. Occasionally the early church even forbade a restored adulterer to "resume the cohabitation of marriage."[11] Sometimes it permanently barred persons from return to office in the church.

Now, it may be necessary to exercise discretion in appointing restored persons to office, just as in the appointment of new converts to office. Such appointment should be by virtue of spiritual fitness, not automatic reappointment. However, it is inconsistent with forgiveness to hold truly restored members in a state of perennial disgrace. It is inconsistent with forgiveness to make them "pay" with continued humiliation or to put them on any other "probation" than that under which all believers live all the time.

The restoration discussed here is the readmission to fellowship of a formerly excommunicated person. Earlier we noted that excommunication calls for the participation of the church. For the same reason, an excommunicated individual's restoration to spiritual fellowship calls for congregational recognition. This is not just to invest the forgiveness with congregational authority, but to inform all the members of the real change of relationship taking place between a readmitted individual and themselves. This allows them to offer the restored person appropriate welcome and support.

There is not, however, one kind of forgiveness sought by admonition and another by the more drastic means of excommunication and restoration. There is only one gospel, and it offers only one kind of spiritual life. Hence in the readmission of excommunicated persons, as in all other aspects of the life of the church, forgiveness must be the only kind of forgiveness the gospel knows—the kind that issues in the discipled life.

7

ADDRESSING THE TASK
"You Who Are Spiritual"

Church discipline is of one piece with the church's
preaching and living of the gospel in the world.
Under no circumstances may we neglect the responsibility of
reaching out with help to people in spiritual trouble.

"Brethren, if a man is overtaken in any trespass, you who are spiritual should restore him in a spirit of gentleness. Look to yourself, lest you too be tempted. Bear one another's burdens, and so fulfill the law of Christ," writes Paul (Gal. 6:1-2).

It is safe to say that the recovery of a faithful, healthy, and effective church discipline will not be easy. The church suffers from a kind of paralysis resulting from an inner ambivalence. The church's desire to observe a biblical precept is countered by the fear of repeating the mistakes of the past. This book has attempted to remove some fears and thus clear the way for obedience to the teaching of Jesus.

Identifying the Whole Task

The introduction to this book served notice that its focus was "emergency spiritual care." As stated there, "The church can and must have recourse to corrective discipline where self-discipline breaks down. Isolating such a subject for special attention does not at all imply that we lose sight of other tasks of the church. [Rather,] the comprehensive view enables us to recover a healthy practice of corrective church discipline."

It is important to repeat here that "discipline is not [just] an extraordinary procedure called into action in extreme circumstances, but part of an ongoing process of helping people in the church grow into Christ's likeness."[1] We are "to grow in grace and in the knowledge of our Lord and Savior Jesus Christ," says the apostle Peter (2 Pet. 3:18). In the words of Paul, "Let the peace of Christ rule in your hearts . . . as you teach and admonish one another in all wisdom, and as you sing psalms and hymns and spiritual songs with thanksgiving in your hearts to God" (Col. 3:15-16). "This kind of formative discipline ought to happen every time the church meets, and even between."[2]

There are two connotations to the word *discipline*. For many people its first connotation is negative, as when a teacher sends a naughty pupil to the principal's office. But its first connotation should be positive, as when a basketball player or musician accepts the discipline of practice. Good students accept the discipline of study. Good business executives accept the discipline of the workplace.

The disciplines of ordinary life such as those just mentioned are usually not considered onerous but welcome, even exhilarating. Through them people achieve a performance and fulfillment they otherwise could not reach.

We do not, for that matter, have to think only of strenuous discipline. Relaxed or "laid-back" disciplines are some of the most important ones, whether or not we think of them as disciplines. A home where parents do not yell at the children, where the children do not hit each other, where everyone can negotiate who gets the car tonight, where teenagers do not "borrow" each others things without asking, where people show up for work or appointments—that is itself discipline and not just the fruit of discipline.

Discipline is not primarily an extraordinary procedure but part of healthy life. Several points about this deserve mention by way of elaboration. First, the church's main time and energy should go into what one writer calls the "formative" kind of discipling. It is only right and proper that the church should give major attention to study, fellowship, worship, mutual aid, visitation, and the "building up of the body of Christ." The church is the place where people learn to care about each other.

As in the relationships of a home and family, the church recognizes that affirmation of the good is much better than criticism of the bad. The church is in the business of realizing human community. It cultivates on both individual and corporate levels the fruit of the Spirit: love, joy, peace, patience, kindness, goodness, faithfulness, gentleness, and self-control (Gal. 5:22).

Second, formative discipling is the best way—if not the only way—to prevent cases from arising that require corrective discipline. At least it will keep them to a minimum. The type of home just described is one that would likely see the fewest instances of problem behavior. Wise instruction, encouragement, and support long before big problems arise can prevent the big problems from arising altogether. To help a struggling family with financial management can forestall an unethical adventure into bad checks. Church seminars about TV and sex may save many Christians a bad trip into sexual immorality.

Third, formative discipling is the best if not the only way to prepare for instances of corrective discipline and to make it effective when it becomes necessary. "Without ongoing training in godly behavior, catastrophe discipline is likely to be fruitless."[3] The truth of this ought to be fairly obvious. The church can invite believers to continue in the Christian way or restore them to it only if there is a recognized Christian way to which it can call them! The church must teach this way so that people can understand it, so it has a chance to again win their allegiance.

Also, people will return to the Christian way successfully only if they are corrected in a truly Christian manner. It is a matter of means and ends. The church will realize the end of Christian discipleship only if the means is the Christian gospel, a point made repeatedly in the preceding pages.

Fourth, what we are calling formative and corrective discipling do not have a clear line between them. We have distinguished between them only in order to speak of critical situations that call for outside help—situations where self-discipline seems to have broken down. For example, we often cannot and need not tell in advance whether some woman's absence from church for several weeks signals a danger of loss of spiritual life. Her neighbor's timely inquiry may mean we will never find out. And so we will also never be able to tell whether that alert inquiry was formative discipling or corrective discipling.

We may understandably identify assault with a knife, incestuous child abuse, or burglary right away as "red flag" critical situations calling for the church's action. However, we don't have to wait to see if a potential problem is going to become an emergency case.

Formative and Corrective Discipling

What we are calling formative and corrective or emergency discipline are of one piece. Addressing crisis situations if the church has not first, and regularly, taught the Christian way would not make sense. Conversely, offering instruction in the Christian walk but not giving attention to the stumbling saint also does not make sense. One should not emphasize or practice either at the expense of the other.

To use again the illustration of physical health, it makes most sense to work at preventive and crisis medicine together. It is foolish to neglect the rules of nutrition and exercise only to rush to the hospital in an emergency. It is also inconsistent to keep the health rules but then refuse to get help in a health crisis. If we desire a healthy life, then we want both health rules *and* emergency care.

Emergency care of people in spiritual danger still seems unpleasant to some, even though it is truly the essence of love and compassion. Some idealistic people would hope to eliminate the need of any corrective discipline. "If only we did a good enough job of Christian preaching and teaching! We might all be so well self-disciplined that we would not have *any* cases needing corrective discipline," they say. Or, "Everyone should take care of their own problems!"

Such an idealistic suggestion calls for a twofold answer. First, it is unrealistic. There are always bound to be some critical cases requiring emergency treatment. Second, self-discipline is, in fact, the goal of all corrective discipline. Corrective discipling intends to return people to self-discipline.

In physical health, crisis intervention for accident injuries, heart attacks, or cancer works toward returning people to their normal lives. The goal is leaving the hospital and returning to normalcy. It is not to keep people forever in the doctor's office or hospital!

That is what corrective discipline is like in the spiritual realm. That is why it is integrally related to normal self-discipline. We emphasize maximal spiritual health to keep spiritual crises to a minimum. When special spiritual help is needed, its goal is to return people to normal spiritual health.

This book has tried to redeem the term *church discipline* by showing its continuity with all discipling. That is, *corrective church discipline is of one piece with the church's preaching and living of the gospel in the world.* If the term *discipline* still bothers us, we can find another one, but *under no circumstance may we neglect the responsibility of reaching out with help to people in spiritual trouble.*

Congregational discipline is the act of discipling an erring brother or sister. According to Matthew 18 going to the sister or brother is a function of the gospel analogous to evangelism or missionary proclamation. Receiving discipline is like receiving the good news as a non-Christian. A person is presented the opportunity of being liberated from the power of sin by coming under the rule of Christ and walking in his way.

At stake is nothing less than the life of the church itself. This is not intended simply as startling rhetoric. It has become an accepted article of recent theology to consider evangelism as part of the essence of the life of the church. Evangelism is not just a desirable but optional task. Unfortunately, congregational discipline has not yet been granted that position.

Discipline and Evangelism

Congregational discipline belongs to the essence of the church as much as evangelism does because both are inescapable implications of the gospel. It makes no sense to declare the good news of liberation from sin to people outside the church and then refuse to declare it to Christians within the church. The gospel is not merely the good news which converts the sinner. It is also the good news by which the Christian can continue to live.

In practice also it makes no sense to accept the task of evangelism and then to neglect discipline. What is the point of adding people to the church through gospel proclamation if membership in that church becomes meaningless because of the failure of discipline? Evangelism itself is soon undermined if people discover that belonging or not belonging to the church makes no difference. The result is the absence of ethical integrity in the church's life. As one writer says,

> The church which neglects to speak the word of judgment will eventually discover that the forgiveness which it speaks is empty and irrelevant to a world which watches the life of the church with discernment.[4]

If a church's aggressive evangelism lacks supporting discipline, the purpose of evangelism shifts. Rather than incorporating people into the discipled life of the church, such evangelism makes conversion a religious experience for its own sake. We see this sort of thing in modern revivalism when many people—most of them already members of some church—go through periodic "conversions." These conversions carry little meaning beyond a temporary emotional charge. If persons are already members of a church, what else does conversion mean?

Some might still ask, Isn't revivalism consistent with the thesis that congregational discipline is a function of the gospel? The answer is that much modern revivalism is organized along parachurch lines. Since it functions primarily outside the congregation, it fails to take seriously the most basic gospel requirement—namely, the ethically accountable life of the church. Proclaiming the gospel means calling people into that community which accepts the rule of God.

It is clear, then, that congregational discipline is essential to the life of the church. Without it the church ceases to have meaning, and without a meaningful church, evangelism also loses its meaning. It is clearly a mistake to believe as some do that ever more aggressive evangelism will make up for the neglect of discipline and its consequent weakening of the church. Ever bigger and better televangelism or crusades will not solve the problem of sin in the church. The more worldly the church, the greater is the danger of big crusades becoming a farce.

The parallel we have shown between gospel proclamation and congregational discipline implies that they are equally indispensable to the realization of the reign of God. In the light of this we can insist that the recovery of discipline according to the gospel will actually strengthen the mission of the church. Evangelism will become clear when people see that conversion leads to a discipled life in the church. Faithful discipline will benefit the outreach of the church.

No doubt some people will protest that an attempt to recover this ministry of discipling will lead back to the legalism and harshness that characterized so much of the church's history. This can happen, of course, but only if discipline ceases to ground itself in the gospel. The alternative to legalism has too often been crass individualism, freedom from any authority of the church. When self-indulgent freedom is put forward as the answer to legalism, it shows that people have not yet caught sight of the gospel. It is not acceptable to pit one against the other and to say that individualism is no worse than legalism. Neither legalism nor individualism provides persons with true liberation from sin. The real options are the liberation of people through the gospel or their continued bondage to sin in the form of *either* individualism or legalism.

A recovery of discipline does not imply a new era of the inquisition. Where it has neglected discipline the church may have to face a backlog of problems. Where a congregation exercises discipline properly, however, its effect is to reduce the need for corrective discipline. This is true wherever a congregation keeps the meaning of discipleship clearly in view.

It is like discipline in a home, says one writer. "We may say of a Christian congregation that it is well-disciplined, not when perpetually engaged in efforts to reclaim offenders, but when there are few offenders to be reclaimed."[5] Corrective discipline is not to be desired for its own sake, of course. But if sin makes its appearance, discipline is very much to be desired as the answer to the problem.

Too many people think that congregational discipline is an embarrassment to the church, and therefore prefer to hide cases of discipline. The serious embarrassment, however, is failure to help an erring Christian. What is embarrassing about offering thieves liberation from a practice that cheats them out of the kind of life God intends? And if they refuse such liberation, what is embarrassing about reminding them honestly that such conduct is incompatible with life in the kingdom of God? Such integrity becomes at this stage the only avenue to their liberation.

People will not consider congregational discipline a disgrace if they see it carried out redemptively instead of punitively. Recall that Jesus' invitation to tax collectors and sinners was an attempt to reclaim people excommunicated from the synagogue. Surely his call to discipleship is not an embarrassment or disgrace! On the contrary, it issues in joy and celebration, as we see from the parable of the prodigal son. That is what it can and should be in our churches, too.

Practical First Steps

You may have heard of the Irishman who, when asked for directions by a traveler, replied, "You can't get there from here." Many churches see the need for a ministry of discipling but believe they can't start from where they are because their church is no longer a spiritual body. That does seem to be the prerequisite according to Galatians 6:1-2. Consider the following suggested steps:

(1) *Begin with a study of the meaning of the Christian life.* There must be some understanding of the norm by which we are to measure our Christian lives. There must be some standard by which to recognize critical cases. Beyond this a congregation, and preferably also denomination, should want to identify risk or danger areas in our society that should receive special attention. Such a task will be difficult because we must go beyond shallow definitions and stereotypes. We must not, however, define spiritual life in terms of an increased number of commandments. Rather, we must sharpen our spiritual sensibility to get a feel for the spirit of life in Christ as portrayed in the Sermon on the Mount.

At the same time the church, too, must prepare itself to decide what specific things it will say "no" to. The apostle Paul held some behaviors to be incompatible with the Christian confession. "Those who do such things,"he says, "will not inherit the kingdom of God" (1 Cor. 6:9).

(2) *Establish meaningful membership in your congregation.* The principle of responsible membership has fallen on hard times in modern America. Beginning in the 1800s, revivalism and missionary movements and a string of parachurch move-

ments have fostered an amorphous, free-floating Christianity that does not need church membership. Televangelists, religion publishers, seminary professors, religious agency executives—to what congregation do they belong? Where are they answerable for their ethical decisions? Recent scandals in these parachurch organizations have shown the consequences of non-accountability. The parachurch image of Christianity has by now replaced the earlier centrality of congregational life. This has furthered the notion that the only accountability needed is within one's own private conscience.

The Mennonite church has a tradition of asking new members of the church at baptism (or joining by transfer) whether they are prepared to "give and receive counsel." This is one of the conditions of their life in the congregation. Such an understanding must be part of any Christian's membership in the church.

Appended to this chapter is a sample of the congregational covenant of my own church. Every congregation should have such a covenant and take it seriously as the basis for every baptism or membership transfer.

Where congregational life has deteriorated badly, meaningful membership might begin with a covenant renewal in which all members commit or recommit themselves to living faith (2 Cor. 13:5). It ought not, of course, take several months to notice a member's absence. A recent church membership study showed that church members are much more likely to continue attending if someone contacts them within the first week or two of their absence.

Meaningful or authentic church membership includes more than attendance, of course. But many congregations would get a helpful start by establishing reasonable expectations about attendance at worship. "In every church I have pastored," writes one pastor, "I have insisted that very meticulous attendance records be maintained on every parishioner . . . because attendance is a good barometer of a person's spiritual condition."[6]

One time this pastor proposed to remove a member's name from the membership rolls who had been nonresident for thirteen years. The man's mother asked, "But who will bury him when he dies?"

"I assured her I would bury her son if necessary," this pastor wrote, "but that we were more concerned about his spiritual welfare now and wanted to prod him to activity in a local church where he lived, two thousand miles away."[7]

We may not want to go as far as the pastor just quoted proposes. Perhaps we do not need a clause in the requirements of membership that reads, "Any member who does not attend church services or financially support the ministry of this assembly, unless providentially hindered, will be subject to review for dismissal."[8] But it is entirely reasonable to invite and expect nonresident members who have good reasons to retain membership in a home church to keep in contact and report their spiritual involvement to their home congregation at regular intervals.

(3) *Establish a congregational policy for discipling.* This means initially to establish a climate of trust and mutual aid. It means establishing the understanding that concern and counsel are not the same as prying into someone's life. Rather, they represent our desire to see each other grow in grace and in the knowledge of Jesus Christ. It also means studying the ministry of discipling. This study is as serious a study as that by a building or pastoral selection committee. It should issue in specific recommendations for implementation. Discipling is not an esoteric mystery that cannot be learned. Willing Christians can grasp the rules of confidentiality and techniques of tactful inquiry. They can learn this as they do accounting, nursing, sales methods, insurance service, and public school teaching. All these professions require human relations skills.

It means in the second place to establish specific and practical lines of responsibility. It should not take a year before someone notices that a certain individual has no longer been showing up in church. Members "falling through the cracks" is a hazard of large congregations, but the danger of anonymity and invisibility is not insuperable. However, congregations must become willing to re-form their existing structures to meet the needs of their members.

> *We must establish the procedures for discipline before a crisis occurs.* Church members should know they are spiritually accountable in this and other ways. They should know that the whole church is to watch for and carefully treat anything that might damage our spiritual health.[9]

Congregations have committees for stewardship, for Christian education, for outreach. They do not expect religious education to happen by itself. Yet most congregations do not have structures in place to help erring believers. Do they expect it to happen by itself? Congregations must have an understanding of how church members can proceed if they sense that some member is faltering in spiritual life.

We must learn to accept as part of normal church life the ministry of discipling a fellow Christian where this becomes needed. We must accept it in the same way that we do discipling of converts—as part of the ongoing task of the church. Congregations should beware, though, of hasty policies fashioned as a result of the last crisis, such as a church rule designed for deacons caught driving under the influence. Precedent can be instructive, but it shouldn't lure us into formulating policy on the basis of sundry cases. What is needed is a grasp of the basic biblical and theological principles that apply to each situation.

(4) *Take the next need for discipling that arises and carry it through with all the love, sensitiveness, and honesty that you can summon.* Refuse to make excuses out of past neglect or mistakes. The steps of corrective discipling according to the gospel have been spelled out in this book:

> (a) Establish the prerequisite of faithful Christian instruction, regular worship, and mutual aid. Believers can then develop a

strong and healthy spiritual life and keep to a minimum the appearance of critical problems.

(b) Recognize acts or attitudes that are incompatible with the Christian way and therefore signify the possible loss of spiritual life.

(c) Confidentially reach out with help to invite a faltering believer to continue or return to the Christian way.

(d) Persist in bringing the problem to resolution, showing patience and tact in continuing to present the way of Christ to those who do not immediately repent. Forgiveness is the outcome the church always seeks, of course. However, the church must be prepared to remove a person from the membership of the church if that becomes inevitable.

(e) Offer joyful restoration at whatever stage a person repents and returns to the obedience of faith.

One congregation showed commendable imagination in a case of corrective discipling in their church. One man who had left their congregation returned in genuine penitence after five years of estrangement. "They literally gave him a new sport coat, had a gold ring made for his finger, and celebrated with him over a veal dinner!"[10] This congregation, as most readers will recognize, took its cue from the story of the prodigal son. That story—and the other ones in Luke 15 about the lost sheep and lost coin—should shape our concept and practice of church discipline.

Addendum
College Mennonite Church Covenant

Introduction
1. We, the College Mennonite Church, are a voluntary community of faith in God whose authority and grace are revealed in the Scriptures and supremely in Jesus Christ, his Son.

2. We are debtors to the whole Christian tradition, but acknowledge our unique debt and commitment to the Anabaptist-Mennonite heritage.

3. We seek by the power of the Spirit to follow Christ in partnership with other congregations of common purpose throughout the world, beginning with Indiana-Michigan Conference and Mennonite General Assembly.

4. We state the following affirmations and intentions as our guidelines and incentives for working together in discerning the mind of Christ for us today.

Our Common Affirmations
5. We affirm that God is always at work calling and forming a people to continue his work of bringing reconciliation and wholeness to all persons. God's supreme act brought Jesus to live as a suffering servant, to offer himself as our Savior, and to rise and reign forever as Lord.

6. We witness in baptism to our surrender to Jesus as Lord, to our adoption into God's family, and to the gift of the Holy Spirit.

7. We affirm that Christ by his Spirit overcomes our separateness and unites us into one body—interdependent, mutually supportive, and accountable to each other.

8. We witness to the power and victory of God's kingdom over the powers of evil as the Holy Spirit creates in us spiritual worship, trust for each other, faithful discipleship, and joyful witness.

My Personal Covenant With the College Mennonite Church

9. To give reality and substance to these affirmations which I hold in common with the sisters and brothers of this congregation,

> *I covenant with them in mutual trust and accountability to give and receive counsel as together we seek to bring all of life under the lordship of Christ.*

This covenant, I believe, calls for continuing primary relationships with at least several other members as we seek together to be faithful disciples of Christ.

Areas of Search and Growth Together

By the grace of God and with the help of sisters and brothers, I will:

10. Participate responsibly in congregational worship, study, fellowship, and decision-making, looking upon these experiences as occasions for counsel, forgiveness, nurture, and correction in my pilgrimage with Christ.

11. Share with other members as we seek to discover, affirm, and develop spiritual gifts so that we can each find our place of ministry in this congregation and beyond.

12. Invest my material, personal, and spiritual resources to meet responsibly the needs of my family, the church, and the world, keeping my personal consumption of goods under the disciplines of love and compassion.

13. Be molded by Christ's example of forgiving, accepting, nonresistant, nondiscriminating love as his way to bring peace, hope, reconciliation, and justice to a world torn by hatred, alienation, and violence.

14. Identify new issues which call for prophetic Christian witness, share the "good news" in deed and word in all relationships, and help fulfill our mission to the ... community and the world.

Sources of Strength

15. I view involvement in a local fellowship of believers so crucial to my spiritual integrity and usefulness that I will seek to continue such a responsible relationship in any community to which I may go.

16. I confess, with all God's people, the need of daily forgiveness and renewing grace which will enable me to glorify God and Christ in the church.

PART 2

THE HISTORICAL RECORD

Even if it may not be this week's fad in American theology, something of the nature of church discipline has always been part of the life of the people of God.

The outlines of what Protestant Christianity came to call church discipline derive from Ezra, the reputed founder of the synagogue. After the deportation and dispersion, Israel was no longer politically independent. She became a "church" with a synagogue pattern of life. Under these circumstances the chief instruments for dealing with violators of Jewish law were banishment and confiscation of property. "And thus began the practice, continued through the Christian centuries, of . . . excommunication."[1]

In the centuries following Ezra, talmudic Judaism developed and refined discipline. Though it may never have operated rigidly and uniformly, the Talmud did describe how the system of discipline functioned.

First and least severe was a rebuke or censure called a *nezifah.* Rabbis usually employed this in cases of disrespect for their authority. According to the Babylonian Talmud, the *nezifah* was effective for one day. According to the Palestinian Talmud, it was effective for seven days. For that period of time the person standing under this censure had to go to his home and to refrain from business or entertainment. He was not to appear in the sight of the rabbi who had pronounced the rebuke over him.

A more serious sentence was the *niddui*. It is sometimes compared to what in the Middle Ages was minor excommunication. It was preceded by three warnings. Its pronouncement always included the words, "May that man live in separation." According to the Babylonian Talmud its duration was seven days, according to the Palestinian, thirty. The Talmud lists twenty-four offenses punishable by this excommunication, mostly insubordination to Mosaic law or its authoritative rabbinic interpretation and application.

The subject of this ban was to don a mourning habit. He was to refrain from bathing, from cutting his hair, and from wearing shoes or sandals. No one was to eat with him, and others were forbidden contact with him, except for his wife and children. He did not count in the ritual number of heads of households necessary for prayers. If he died while under the ban, a special stone placed on his grave reminded everyone of the fact. Furthermore, his relatives were forbidden to rend their garments or to engage in the customary practices of mourning.

An individual who remained incorrigible after three *nidduis* fell under the *cherem*, the curse. According to one authority this curse could be imposed only in the presence of ten members of the community, the minimum complement needed to form a synagogue. At this excommunication people would extinguish lights or carry a symbolic coffin out of the house, as in a funeral rite, symbolizing that the subject of the ban was dead, cut off from Israel and from Israel's spiritual life.

Serious as this ban was, it was not irrevocable. When the individual reformed, the ban could be revoked by the appropriate authorities.[2]

Discipline in the New Testament

The idea of church discipline in the New Testament comes out of the practice of Judaism just described. The words of

Jesus in Matthew 18 follow quite closely a passage in the *Testament of the Twelve Patriarchs*, Gad 6:3, 7.

> Love ye one another from the heart; and if a man sin against thee, speak peaceably to him, and in thy soul hold not guile; and if he repent and confess, forgive him. . . . And if he be shameless and persist in his wrongdoing, even so forgive him from the heart, and leave to God the avenging.[3]

Besides the basic text in Matthew 18:15-17 and its parallel in Luke 17:3, many other passages in the New Testament treat this subject. We have already discussed most of these. The story of Ananias and Sapphira in Acts 5 shows an instance of dealing with sin in the early Christian community. In Romans 16:17 Paul advises avoidance of those who cause dissension. In 1 Corinthians 5 he explicitly directs the excommunication of an obdurate offender. In 2 Corinthians 2:5-9 he encourages the readmission of an excommunicated person. In Galatians 6:1 he asks those who are spiritual to restore someone overtaken in a trespass. In 2 Thessalonians 3:6, 14 he instructs his readers to avoid idlers and anyone who refuses to obey. Finally, the pastoral letters refer to avoidance of the disobedient, hypocrites, and factious (2 Tim. 3:2-5; Titus 3:10).

A systematic discussion of discipline in the New Testament would require another book. Formulating a theology of discipline from the New Testament means more, however, than reading a selected group of texts. Under the pressure of immediate cases, people too often use the texts just mentioned as rules and policies. They assume that one can use these for any similar assortment of moral contingencies. They thus devise a scheme for "codifying sins and tariffing sentences."[4]

The Development of Penance

With regard to the development of church discipline in the history of Christendom, one historian thinks it striking how in the sparse literature which has appeared concerning the office of the keys and church discipline, again and again writers hurriedly turn from the New Testament to the Reformers. In this way their orientation is determined by an attitude toward Rome.[5]

The comment advises us not to overlook the intervening era, which has much to teach us—positively as well as negatively. It has definitely had an influence upon modern church life—indirectly by way of Protestant reaction, if nothing else.

In the postapostolic period of the first two or three centuries, discipline was a prominent concern of the church. The debate over the possibility of forgiveness for post-baptismal sin makes this clear, as does the formation of categories of mortal sins. The problems raised by the persecutions in the third century made this more acute. How *should* the church deal with the lapsed (persons who had denied the faith under persecution) who were genuinely penitent? The central issue in this era was whether excommunicated persons could be reinstated in the church, and if so, under what conditions.

The penitential system apparently developed gradually during the third century. In the *Apostolic Constitutions*, a treatise of A.D. 252-270 from Syria,[6] there is a fairly full description of an early stage of the emerging penitential system. These constitutions instruct the bishop as follows:

> When you see the offender in the congregation, you are to take the matter heavily, and to give orders that he be expelled from it. Upon his expulsion, the Deacons are likewise to express their concern, to follow and to find the party, and to detain him for awhile without the Church. In a little time they are to come back, and to intercede with you on his behalf . . . as our Saviour interceded with His Father for sinners, saying, as we learn from the Gospel, "Father, forgive them; for they know not what they do." Then you shall order him to be brought into the Church; and after having examined whether he be truly penitent, and fit

to be readmitted into full Communion, you shall direct him to continue in a state of mortification for the space of two, three, five, or seven weeks, according to the nature of the offense; and then, after some proper admonitions, shall dismiss [or absolve] him.[7]

A person under penance engaged in symbolic acts of repentance until the bishop restored him. These acts included wearing sackcloth and ashes, weeping at the door of the church, and interceding with the elders for readmission.

There were no grades or stages of penitents here yet, and the duration of penance was still relatively brief. The Canons of Elvira (c. A.D. 305) also do not yet mention penitential stations.[8] But in the fourth century some churches identified three or four stations of penance through which excommunicated penitents were to pass. These were part of the rigorous system usually associated with the church order of this era.

First the offender was excommunicated for mortal sin. Then he made confession to a presbyter. This presbyter then admitted him to penance and assigned the forms of public penance through which he was to move (the stations of hearer, kneeler, and stander). Finally the penitent was absolved by the bishop in a public liturgy preceding Easter communion. The Council of Ancyra in Galatia in A.D. 314 alluded to these stations as " 'the defined grades.' The system [was] an accepted system; and [was] acquiring a technical terminology."[9]

About this time also the church fixed the duration of penance. Basil, bishop of Caesarea in the middle of the fourth century, outlined the church's requirements. For example, such persons as were guilty of fornication or adultery were for the first year

> excluded entirely from the whole service, and were to stand weeping at the church door, which was the Station of mourners; in the year following, they were admitted to that of hearers; in the third to that of the Prostrate, called [properly]

the penance; in the fourth they were permitted to stand with
the faithful whilst they communicated, but might not themselves partake with them. And this I have termed the Station of
. . . "bystanders"; and thus, at last, they were restored in full to
all their privileges, and were allowed to communicate.[10]

Although the terms of penance were spelled out in detail,
they varied according to the different canonical books.
Gradually the terms grew more severe even while (and perhaps
because) their effectiveness diminished, especially in the
Eastern part of the church. "At the same time, and by the very
same degrees, [as] the efficacy and power of [discipline] declined, the forms and show of it increased and multiplied."[11]

"Not till the end of the third century was a rigorous and
fixed system of penitential discipline established," one historian
remarks. "And then this could hardly maintain itself a
century."[12] Still another historian says, in summary, "It would
appear that the practice of public penance nowhere died out,
but that it ceased to be the practice of the main stream of offending Christians."[13]

When we review the penance of this era, what do we discover to be its main features? For one thing, the church took
sin seriously, although it apparently restricted its focus to the
three cardinal sins: murder, unchastity, and idolatry. Second,
there was a strong distinction between church and world, in the
light of which excommunication and penance carried much
weight.

Unfortunately, however, there is little mention of admonition within the Christian community in this era or of attempts
to save offenders through preventive counsel.

The Advent of Celtic Penance

In the later Middle Ages the meaning and structure of discipline practice shifted in a major way through the influence of
a system of confession that arose in British Christianity. In the
words of the historian Watkins:

> It is one of the most remarkable facts of Church history that never at any time did the continental system of public penance gain a foothold in these [British] islands. . . . They had an important monastic system with many peculiar features, and in connexion with this monastic system they developed a procedure of Penance, which not only held the field as regards the British Isles, but was destined to meet and to supersede the existing penitential procedure of the continent.[14]

Sometimes called the Celtic penitential system, this penance originated in the vigorous spiritual life of the early Irish monasteries. There monks voluntarily confessed their sins and problems to each other in order to receive forgiveness and spiritual counsel.

The Celtic penitential system was considerably different from the earlier Latin one. The Latin penitential discipline was the method for a person to regain entrance into the church after having been excommunicated for one of the cardinal sins. It was a public penance. In theory it was unrepeatable, at least till the Third Council of Toledo, A.D. 389.[15]

In contrast, the Celtic penitential was a periodic private confession within the monastic community. Later, in the parish system, confessors spoke to a parish priest. Neither the confession nor the penance imposed (fasting, prayers, alms) was necessarily public. Nor did it require a special appearance at public worship. Furthermore, the absolution was not a matter of public liturgy, for the priest absolved in private. Moreover, the priest eventually came to pronounce absolution before the satisfaction of penance instead of after. The Latin penance was one people avoided, since it signified the humiliation of a fall and of excommunication. The Celtic was one people sought, since it signified the virtue of piety and forestalled excommunication.

The Celtic system came from the British Isles to the continent, chiefly under Charles the Great through the British scholars he brought to his court. It is not surprising that this system in due time prevailed throughout the Catholic Church. Already at the Council of Chalon, held sometime between A.D. 639 and 654, the bishops present expressed the judgment that "the Penance of sinners . . . we deem to be useful for all men."[16] The Dialogue of Egbert, Archbishop of York from 732 to 736, speaks of the custom of laity as well as clergy going to confession each year in the twelve days before Christmas. This custom practically carried the force of law. Mandatory annual confession eventually became canon law at the Fourth Lateran Council in 1215

> Every *fidelis* [believer] of either sex shall after the attainment of years of discretion confess his sins with all fidelity to his own priest at least once in the year. Otherwise let him during life be repelled from entering the Church and when dead let him lack Christian burial.[17]

Actually the change in penitential practice of which we are speaking was not simply a replacement of the Latin system by the Celtic. To some extent and for some time the two coexisted in the church. One historian observes that after the seventh century the ordinances ("capitularies") of the Frankish kings made the following special provision:

> If anyone had made a private and voluntary confession, he should do penance in private, while if he had made a public and open confession, he should also openly before the Church do penance in accordance with the canonical grades of penance.[18]

The two systems did not, however, simply continue to co-exist. "Public penance gradually grew rare and came to be known as solemn penance," imposed only for notorious and scandalous crimes.[19] Also, as the decree of the Fourth Lateran Council shows, failure to follow the new requirement of repeated private confession carried the risk of excommunication. So the old Latin and Celtic systems in effect stratified into the great and small ban, major and minor excommunication. They thus became grades of severity in the church's evolving system of dealing with its offenders.

In retrospect, the most significant development in this era was the confusion between the church and the world, between church discipline and secular law, a confusion that began with the Constantinian era. Since membership in the church became coterminous with citizenship in the state, church discipline became confused with secular law, as seen from Elisabeth Vodola's book, *Excommunication in the Middle Ages.*[20]

Reformation Ventures

For the Protestant Reformers church discipline was, in the words of one historian, "no incidental question."[21] Luther wrote one treatise on the power of the keys and another on the breakdown of the unity and authority of the church and the resultant uncertainty about the validity of the ban. As one scholar asserts, "Only ignorance or thoughtlessness can claim that the motif of church discipline was foreign to Luther."[22] Nevertheless, Luther never formally instituted an order for church discipline. The first *Kirchenordnung* (church polity) of Wittenberg in 1533 contains no instructions for penance, confession, or the ban.

As late as 1540 Luther considered an organized venture, but it did not materialize. He himself gives the reason: "I would gladly institute it, but it's not the time for it yet." The rationalization behind this statement is curious indeed: "If only there were people who would allow themselves to be disciplined!" However, that was not the only reason, perhaps not even the chief one. Despite his hesitation to inaugurate a formal discipline, Luther sporadically and almost recklessly practiced it himself and called upon other Lutheran leaders to do likewise.[23]

A more important restraining influence was his fear that the Reformation church would fall back into the evils of the Catholic ban, or major excommunication. Luther had already rejected this ban with its civil penalties by 1537.[24] Hence the discipline emerging in the earliest Lutheran tradition emphasized the role of preaching, with exclusion from communion as the final resort. "According to the evangelical Lutheran view the central point of church discipline is exclusion from the sacraments; discipline is above all a discipline of the Lord's Supper."[25]

Unfortunately, Luther was not consistent with himself. On several occasions he advocated that an individual banned from the Lord's Supper who did not respond to the ban be given over to the secular authorities and exiled. As his rejection of the Catholic ban shows, Luther saw the problems of such a relation of church and state. Although he avoided such a relation in theory, he nevertheless furthered it practically by his refusal to institute a church discipline.[26] At one time, for example, Luther stated that "church discipline would be superfluous if the state would be thorough enough in its law enforcement."[27]

It is not surprising, therefore, that in the post-Reformation period discipline in Lutheran territory fell into the hands of the state by default. This was precisely because Luther had refused to institute a definite church order for it. The consistory, an emergency organization growing out of the practice of visitation, became a permanent government-related organization already in the 1540s. "Melanchthon was the chief agent in preparing the visitation articles by which the government [princes] surveyed every parish in Electoral Saxony and supervised religious and moral life."[28] Hence what came out of the Reformation on this score was just the opposite of what Luther intended in his original insight and position.

The eventual pattern was that a minister could exclude people from communion. Beyond that the consistory reserved the right to excommunicate, impose fines, or otherwise punish offenders.[29] The return to this pattern was in effect a return to the great ban of the pre-Reformation church. With power reverting to the state, the church lost its authority and power to exercise its own proper discipline. Luther's failure to recover an evangelical church discipline is truly unfortunate, since he had recovered the proper basis for it in his doctrine of justification by grace through faith. The righteousness of Christ is the proper basis of all church discipline.

With the advent of German rationalism and the enlightenment, practically all discipline ceased. In some parts of Germany the state even began specifically to forbid certain forms of discipline and to restrict the powers of the church.[30]

In contrast to Lutheran hesitancy in discipline the churches of the Reformed tradition in southern Germany and Switzerland boldly instituted it. Reformed theology made church discipline one of the marks of the church, along with right preaching of the gospel and proper administration of the sacraments. Calvin himself however, did not "make discipline an explicit mark of the church."[31]

What is most notable about the system that developed under Zwingli and Martin Bucer is the church's intentional use of the secular authorities. For them the Christian magistrates functioned as elders within the church in the execution of discipline. Zwingli reserved the right of excommunication to magistrates, as the First and Second Helvetic Confessions point out. This state of affairs reflected Zwingli's theory: "The preaching office is the guiding spirit, the authorities (*die Obrigkeit*) the executive organ of the state church organism.[32]

In 1525

> a tribunal was created consisting of two secular priests, two members of the larger council, and two members of the smaller council, but this institution was still far removed from an organization of the ecclesiastical congregation; it simply reported its findings to the secular authority.[33]

Of the major Reformers the systematic Calvin was the one
who went furthest in the implementation of discipline. He de-
voted a chapter to discipline in the fourth book of *The Institutes*. In it he says:

> As the saving doctrine of Christ is the soul of the Church, so dis-
> cipline forms the ligaments which connect the members to-
> gether, and keep each in its proper place. Whoever, therefore,
> desire either the abolition of all discipline, or obstruct its res-
> toration, whether they act from design or inadvertency, they
> certainly promote the entire dissolution of the Church.[34]

Calvin made acceptance of discipline a condition of his
return to Geneva in 1541. In his establishment of the consistory
of twelve men, according to the *Ordonnances*, he insisted upon
the church's independence from the civil authorities.

In actuality this independence was not strictly maintained,
for the magistrates were to supply political support for the
church, as in Zwingli's Zurich. The Gallican Confession held
that God appointed magistrates to suppress crimes against the
first *and* second table of the decalogue. Even when the church
maintained independence, the actual functioning of the consistory was in the nature of a deutero-government. The methods
it employed, such as monetary fines for delinquency in attending church, were often inconsistent with the gospel.[35]

Discipline was also, of course, an important part of the
Anabaptist movement.[36] It was the second of seven articles
treated in the Schleitheim Confession of 1527:

> We are agreed as follows on the ban: The ban shall be em-
> ployed with all those who have given themselves to the Lord, to
> walk in His commandments, and with all those who are
> baptized into the one body of Christ and who are called
> brethren or sisters, and yet who slip sometimes and fall into er-
> ror and sin, being inadvertently overtaken. The same shall be
> admonished twice in secret and the third time openly dis-

ciplined or banned according to the command of Christ. Matthew 18. But this shall be done according to the regulation of the Spirit before the breaking of bread, so that we may break and eat one bread, with one mind and in one love, and may drink of one cup.[37]

Unfortunately, Anabaptist practice did not match the ideal. "In spite of the repeated emphasis of the early Swiss leaders to practice the ban only in sincere Christian love, the potential punitive implications of the ban became increasingly problematic after Schleitheim."[38] Menno Simons wrote three tracts on church discipline, especially about the issue of shunning.[39] Pressured by the "hard banners" (people who advocated strict avoidance), Menno became increasingly defensive in these tracts. He tried hard to resist the logic that marital avoidance implies a *de facto* divorce.

Because of their circumstances and convictions, the Anabaptists did not use political power in the exercise of discipline. Interestingly, the Netherlands Anabaptists practiced shunning for some decades. When this practice had about run its course in Dutch Mennonitism, the Amish picked up the practice. These followers of Jacob Amman use various forms of it to this day.

Under their reading of the New Testament, the Church of the Brethren also taught and practiced discipline from the time of their founding under Alexander Mack.[40] "At least part of the impetus for the formation of the Church of the Brethren was the fact that among those radical Pietists who had split from the established churches in Germany, there still seemed to be some need for a disciplined corporate expression of the Christian faith."[41]

The English-Speaking World

In the English-speaking world it was in Scottish Presbyterianism and Puritanism that "the rigorous discipline of Ge-

neva found its most genial soil."[42] The Scottish Church
continued the policy of requesting state support begun by the
Reformed Church on the continent. According to the
seventeenth-century Scottish divines, "It is [the Christian
magistrate's] most solemn duty to support the ministry in its
exercise of the 'key of discipline' by every means in its
power."[43]

Fortunately, Puritanism in England did not have the
political power to use this arrangement, whether or not it
wanted to. Perhaps for that reason Puritanism fashioned a doctrine of church discipline independent of secular authorities.
The Puritan confession of 1589 sets forth its view of discipline
virtually as a paraphrase of Matthew 18. Understandably, the
confession emphasizes the authority of the whole congregation.
Popular opinion often brands the Puritans as legalists. But what
strikes the impartial reader is their concern to follow in their
"watch and care" the directives of the New Testament.[44]

English Baptists practiced discipline conscientiously. John
Smyth held that "the cheef care of every member must be to
watch over his brother . . . in bearing one another's burden . . .
admonishing the unruly, comforting the feeble-mynded . . .
admonishing the excommunicate . . . restoring them that are
fallen." At whatever point someone under discipline showed
repentance, "the procedure came to an end." The only cause
for excommunication was "[despising] the counsel of the
church."[45]

In general, English Baptists viewed discipline "in a highly
positive light." They did not see it as intruding upon their
private lives but as seeking their general well-being. "In fact it
was considered 'disorderly' for anyone in the church to contract
a debt before having applied to the church for relief."[46] For
that reason one congregation stipulated "that the members of
everie Church or Congregation ought to knowe one another
. . . so they may performe all the duties of love one towards
another both to soule and bodies. . . . And therefore a Church

ought not to consist off such a multitude as cannot have a particular knowledge one of another."[47] This timely word of counsel many American Baptist congregations might heed.

Methodism at its outset had a vigorous discipline. The societies are to be commended for the primary emphasis they gave to positive spiritual counsel, which resulted in the sanctified lives of their members. At the same time they also had recourse, where necessary, to corrective measures.

An ambiguity arose in Methodist discipline by virtue of its relation to Anglicanism. For those who were expelled from the societies fell back into the broad bosom of the Anglican Church, with which Wesley always remained connected. This inevitably suggested that the disciplined life of the societies was not in the end normative, but rather a counsel of perfection as in the pre-Reformation church. When Methodism later became an independent communion, Wesleyan practice was translated into church discipline, especially in America.[48]

Freedom to exercise church discipline was one of the implications of the North American free church situation. One study of frontier Methodists, Baptists, and Presbyterians of 1800-1850, mostly of Kentucky and Tennessee, claims that

> no Christian looked upon his behavior as "nobody's business". . . . The members of these pioneer congregations felt both free and obliged to watch over each other. . . . Moreover, at their best the systems of admonition and correction were intended as means of repentance and reconciliation for the fallen. Their investigations were not just snooping; they were devised to protect and to keep from harm."[49]

In one Presbyterian church a committee went to speak with Elvyra Thompson, who had committed adultery. They had received

> instructions to "deal with her in a . . . Christian manner and know the state of her mind and her feelings." They found her

"truly penitent, and manifesting that godly sorrow that worketh life." Thus they "felt bound by the ties of Christian affection to forgive her and restore her to the privileges of Christ's Church again."[50]

A study of pre-Civil War Mississippi and Louisiana Baptist churches shows how church discipline operated in integrated congregations. Members "whose treatment to their slaves is unscriptural" were to be dealt with "according to the rule of the Gospel" (i.e., Matthew 18), recommended the Mississippi Baptist Association in 1808.[51]

"Henry Spencer was banished from the Bethany [MS] Church in August 1858 for 'cruelly beating his slave.' " William West was denied a letter of dismissal (transfer) from the Hephzibah, Louisiana, church in 1819 "because he whipped a 'black brother of the church.' "

"Shall a member be held in fellowship that treats his slaves with barbarity?" asked the Hephzibah Church in 1820. "The answer was in the negative."

"Daniel Edds was accused of abusing one of his slaves. At the March 1823 conference the church severed all ties with Edds." The Palestine, Mississippi, congregation decided in 1834 "to abide by 'the 18th of Matthew as a rule to govern the church by [and] to faithfully and impartially administer [discipline] to black and white, male and female.' "[52]

These Baptist congregations also dealt with many other issues, of course. Among them were debts, gambling, profanity, stealing sheep, wife abuse, absence from church meetings, and physical violence.[53]

Today a free-church situation exists in nearly every non-European part of the world. So-called "mission churches" or "younger churches" often find themselves in a position like that of the primitive church. A recent edition of an encyclopedia of religion devotes a whole section to the discussion of discipline in the younger churches.[54] A German author affirms its necessity in the missionary setting.[55] So does Lesslie Newbigin, a former bishop in the church of South India.

> The Church in a non-Christian cultural environment has to take seriously the business of discipline ... because without this the Church's witness to the non-Christian world becomes hopelessly compromised.[56]

A prominent modern missiologist "has commented that there is a positive correlation between corrective church discipline and church growth, especially in third world countries."[57]

This all-too-sketchy review shows that *church discipline has always been part of the life of the people of God*—at least until recently. Many more studies such as the ones just cited are needed to fill out the historical picture for our understanding and benefit.

THE CONTEMPORARY SCENE

*How a task of the church such as discipling the erring could
reach such reduced visibility as it has today
is truly baffling.*

Today much of the church is in a position similar to that of
early Christianity, a minority in a pagan world. In that sense
church history has come full circle. Given that observation, it is
remarkable that the church has apparently lost interest in the
subject of church discipline in comparison with previous
centuries. Even many nineteenth-century books on the doctrine of the church still discussed discipline in some fashion—as
one of the powers of the church, for example.

The ecumenical movement and the rise of biblical theology
since World War II produced a flood of books on the doctrine
of the church. It is striking, however, that discipline receives
scant treatment in these books. Although many of them discuss
the meaning of the holiness of the church, few specifically
mention discipline as a way of dealing with sin in the church.

Over the centuries the church has used a variety of terms to
describe this function. These terms include *penance, confession, church discipline,* and *the sacrament of reconciliation*
(the current Catholic term). How such a function—maintained
as it was for nearly nineteen hundred years—could reach such
reduced visibility as it has today is truly baffling. Such reduced

interest and visibility did not happen with worship, the sacraments, the ministry, church buildings, theological education, or missions.

The Loss of Church Discipline

Almost two generations ago some voices were already calling for the recovery of a sound and biblical discipline. Emil Brunner wrote:

> The function of Church discipline has ... to a very great extent, fallen into disuse.... The Church ought to know, however, that this absence of any kind of Church discipline inevitably gives the impression that to belong or not to belong to the Church comes to the same thing in the end, and makes no difference in practical life.[1]

A German theologian said:

> Of all the problems that press upon the church today and demand solution I know of none so theologically complicated, and thus none whose solution is so urgent and of such fundamental and far-reaching significance, as the problem of church discipline.[2]

A British writer said:

> [Today] discipline, with its suggestions of hardness and rigidity, is contrasted unfavorably with the New Testament emphasis on love and the Spirit of Christ. But the plain fact is that our Christian life has been impoverished as the result of this lack of proper discipline ... so that instead of helping each other to "grow in grace and in the knowledge of our Lord Jesus Christ," we have been, albeit unconsciously, holding each other back.[3]

We could add to these quotes others from the Presbyterian, Methodist, United Church of Christ, and Southern Baptist traditions as well as from the Mennonite Church.

This broad spectrum shows that concern for discipling the erring is not necessarily the preoccupation of sectarians. These are responsible voices calling the church to reexamine the subject and put into practice whatever such reexamination demands. Many ministers and lay people today share this sense of urgency.

> Church discipline that takes sin seriously is almost extinct (especially in traditional churches) and church morality is often tarnished.[4]

> It is true that, historically, the church has sometimes erred in this matter of discipline, but today the problem is one of outright neglect.[5]

> Church discipline "is one of the least talked about subjects in the church." Many are afraid to discuss it. Most believers would rather talk about victorious Christian living.[6]

> The once-binding church manuals of discipline have all but disappeared from the shelves of churches and pastors' libraries, and the few which remain are certainly not being observed in the life of today's religious constituency. Few seem to know what the Bible says about this pertinent subject and fewer seem to care.[7]

Many people feel that the church should be able to do something about Christians whose lives are threatened with spiritual shipwreck—something more than condemnation or apathy. In the light of church trends and public opinion, however, these concerned Christians are at a loss.

If in fact many responsible Christians share this concern about discipling, perhaps it is time to recognize that discipling is indispensable to the Christian faith. Discipling is part of the gospel. It is an inescapable consequence of the process we call proclamation of the good news of the kingdom of God.

Reasons for the Loss

One of the reasons for the absence of discipling in many quarters today is the reaction of churches to serious mistakes in the past. Remembering discipline for clothing or hairstyles or alleged unorthodox doctrine, they now hesitate to engage in any discipling whatever. One Southern Baptist says, "The over-reaction of most Southern Baptist congregations to the abuses in church discipline in the past have made them very slow to return to the spiritual practice."[8]

This loss of discipling also results from the individualism that has crept into our churches.[9] The church has for some time been experiencing the privatization of religion and its restriction to a very limited sphere. Often Christians themselves have ignorantly fostered this trend. Not a few church members accept the common notion that the church has no business sticking its nose into what they wish to define as their private lives. As a result the church is increasingly losing influence also in public morals.

> Too often now when people join a church, they do so as consumers. If they like the product, they stay. If they do not, they leave. They can no more imagine a church disciplining them than they could a store that sells goods disciplining them. It is not the place of the seller to discipline the consumer. In our churches we have a consumer mentality.[10]

Sometimes North American Christianity has tried to handle the problem of sin in the church through an alternative to discipling—revivalism. Erring and backsliding saints are not discipled. They are "saved" or "brought back to the Lord" at some subsequent revival. The distinction between revivalism and evangelism has long since blurred, a sign of the transfer of the problem of discipling to another arena. Many, if not the majority, of "decisions" at evangelistic services might be more accurately termed restorations. Baptists, Lutherans, Mennonites, Methodists, Presbyterians, even Pentecostals, sign decision cards and return to the faith. Why were they not offered help at the time of their lapse rather than neglected until a revival might restore them?

What is wrong with revivalism as a substitute for discipling? For one thing, it fails to address faltering saints until long after they have left the church. Then, many who have left the church never come to the revivals. Why should the church not go after the wayward, as the good shepherd did for the lost sheep, instead of waiting for them to return home by way of a revival meeting?

For another thing, coliseum crusades are too impersonal to assure follow-up. If someone does personally develop contact with a recommitted disciple, there is no reason why such a discipling ministry could not have happened long before.

Furthermore, restoration after revival fosters and perpetuates the notion that Christian faith is a matter of episodic experience rather than a sustained discipled life. Finally, modern revivalism has taken on a suprachurch life of its own. It fosters the idea that extra-congregational Christianity is normal Christianity.

Revivalism as an American institution has doubtless done much good. However, much revivalism feeds on the pathological syndrome of defective views of church membership. Persons respond at a mass meeting and sign a decision card. A campaign worker likely refers them back to the church where the problem began, a local church that still has not developed an alert ministry of discipling.

One other important related movement in North American religion deserves comment here for its ambiguous influence upon the development of church discipline. It is the holiness-pentecostal-charismatic movement. As we can see from the time of Wesley onward, one of the first purposes of the religious experience stressed in this tradition is holiness. People have used various terms to describe it: deeper life, second blessing, entire sanctification, baptism of the Spirit. One of the first practices usually reinstituted in movements of this tradition is church discipline.

And yet an inherent danger lurks in the emphasis upon a sensational experience as the avenue to such holiness, an experience usually portrayed as one of unqualified happiness, even ecstasy. The focus shifts from the life allegedly made possible by the experience to the experience for its own sake. This may lead to a succession of experiences—rallies, retreats, emotional services. Thus some persons subconsciously begin to accept the experience as a *substitute* for the holy life. This development is undeniably visible in many churches as well as in some religious television shows and parachurch organizations.

Another major reason for the modern decline of church discipline is an increasing concession of such functions to the state. Historically, Reformed theology considered the secular or civil authorities the functionaries of church discipline in their enforcement of the law. Of course, they were to take their guidance from the Word of Christ as preached by the church. When Luther said, "Church discipline would be superfluous if the state would be thorough enough in its law enforcement," he surely expected that the civil authorities would regulate society according to Christian norms. He did not, however, explicitly instruct secular princes to take their cues from the church as did Martin Bucer.

Already in earliest Protestantism the balance of power tilted toward regional secular governments because of the breakdown of the unity of the church. For example, the Zurich city council told Zwingli how far he could go in his reforms. Today the state has become radically secular. By its own admission it does not take its cues from the faith for the governance of society. Time has thus reversed the relationship. If anything, the state now dictates to the church the parameters of the church's authority.

Most Protestants consent with minimal reservations to the

growing monopoly of the secular judicial system. This growing monopoly is a development of grave proportions, and for other issues besides church discipline.[11] For discipline itself, however, the state's aggressiveness in taking over the treatment of offenders has several consequences.

First, it virtually excludes the Spirit of Christ and the option of forgiveness for an offender. The law asks only two questions, Is the defendant guilty? and what is the punishment? Where in our criminal justice system is there scope for forgiveness of sin, the most central theme of the gospel?

Second, it distorts and neglects many Christian values. The state is heavy on property values and practically ignores sexual offenses (except rape), lying (one of the Ten Commandments!), and alcohol abuse. Our judicial systems impose penalties upon a youth who gets into petty theft or upon a woman who shoplifts, but they ignore a person who commits adultery. And yet, which act hurts people more?

Third, the judicial system encroaches upon and restricts churches. Occasionally, as in its rulings on abortion, the state judicial system may not be an expression of the reign of Christ, but quite possibly an obstacle to it.

For reasons such as these, the secular judicial code and criminal justice process are deficient morally from a Christian perspective. One cannot accept them as a substitute for discipling. And yet many Christians unconsciously cherish the notion that the secular authorities will relieve the church of the task of dealing with offenders. If this notion was ever justified, it is less so now than at the time of the Reformation.

Instead of the church informing secular law, secular law shapes the values of the church. Too many Christians accept the moral assumptions of our legal system. The law even begins to define righteousness for them and the way of dealing with unrighteousness. They hesitate to exercise church discipline, but then uncritically embrace the punitive judicial system.

The law has affected church discipline in another respect. In recent years the threat of litigation has given many churches second thoughts about discipling. In some cases aggrieved church members under discipline have taken recourse to the secular courts, sometimes for invasion of privacy.

One immediately notices several ironies in such litigation. First, the secular courts are notorious for the absence, if not violation, of privacy. In that arena there is little protection of privacy. Properly conducted, discipling in most instances offers much better chances of preserving privacy.

Furthermore, where church discipling gets suppressed because of fear of litigation, all people, including those who sue, lose the prospect of help. This is especially true with regard to alcohol or other drug addiction, sexual-marital entanglements, embezzlements, and political scandal. Such people will end up without help, except the "help" of the courts.

Litigation contains a second irony. Those who complain most loudly about the encroachment of the state upon the church's territory are often the least hesitant to sue when that seems to suit their purposes. They often uncritically typify America as a Christian nation, unquestioningly assuming that the judicial system, too, is part of this Christian America. It is puzzling to hear people denounce church discipline and then turn to the secular judicial system.

As two experts point out, litigation in the secular courts is outrageously expensive and usually offers only a win-or-lose outcome. The church, they say, can offer much more sensitivity and nuances of judgment. Above all, it can reconcile and redeem, so all parties can win.[12]

Whether or not the assessment offered here is correct, there *is* a balance which may get tilted by default. Less church discipline will leave a gap or vacuum which the judicial system is only too ready to move into, confident as it is of its omnicompetence. More church discipline competently and tactfully carried out may well reassure our courts—and society in general—that the separation of church and state continue to deserve respect in this matter. The church has a right to set membership standards for those who voluntarily join it. Discipline over such standards is then outside the jurisdiction of the state.

Some writers who have studied the issue of litigation and church discipline offer the following counsel to churches. First, churches should state membership standards very clearly. Second, they should have an established, stated, and understood church discipline policy, which they follow conscientiously. Third, congregations must observe confidentiality scrupulously.[13] Fourth, they should keep accurate written minutes or records (also kept in confidential church files) whenever a discipline case reaches the level of action by elders of a congregation or the whole congregation.[14]

We could add that when a church follows the above guidelines, it may still have to proceed with courage, even with the risk of litigation. Loving church discipline ought to reduce the risk, though. Many people, given a choice, would prefer to fall into the hands of the church than into those of the courts.

Prospects and Problems

Lament over the neglect in church discipling today must be countered by the recognition of much good discipling carried out under another term, pastoral counseling. As one pastor asserts, "Often I hear the complaint that the church is not practicing church discipline any more. This is not true. We who are pastors, elders, deacons, church members are constantly rebuking, exhorting, encouraging, and warning our people— but mostly in private."[15] This faithful labor is effective, even if not visible. Many pastors today receive more instruction and internship experience in the art of counseling than most ministers did in the history of the Christian church.

The values of church discipline in the form of pastoral counseling are qualified, however. Some have borrowed pastoral counseling techniques uncritically from the canons and methods of the secular schools of psychology. Thus, for example, the counselor may seek to help a person resolve guilt feelings without concern for ethical transformation. There is the related risk of not moving beyond counseling to resolution in penitence and forgiveness or excommunication from the church.

One professor says that in biblical counseling

> those involved have discovered that church discipline is an essential tool. . . . Without it there is no way to bring many counseling cases to a satisfactory conclusion. . . . Counseling and church discipline are inextricably intertwined; neither can be carried on effectively and biblically without the other.[16]

In a case of public sin private absolution cannot convey to the offender the needed public congregational forgiveness, acceptance, and expiation of sin. Furthermore, professional private counseling by design or default may unnecessarily limit the role of all lay members of the church. Instead of limiting this ministry of counseling, Christian professionals should equip all members of congregations as much as possible in the skills and ethics of such counseling.

Professor J. Carl Laney provides evidence that church discipline proper still happens today in a survey reported in his book.[17] Of 1,250 questionnaires he mailed to a wide spectrum of pastors from United Methodists to Seventh-Day Adventists, 439 (35 percent) were returned. Laney found that two-thirds of these pastors felt "adequately equipped" and "capable" to deal with church discipline situations. (These were 3 and 4 respectively on a scale of 1-5.)

Respondents reported an average "success" rate (i.e., "restoration") in nearly 52 percent of the cases they had "observed or been involved with." The biggest factor contributing to the neglect of discipline was pastoral anxiety about "personal confrontation." Of actions pastors deemed appropriate for discipline, the five highest were, in order: incest, adultery, child abuse, wife beating, and fornication. The biggest difficulty pastors reported was that "the offender simply leaves the church or transfers churches."

Laney also reported that few churches withhold communion anymore. Two-thirds of the pastors reporting in this survey held that a church leader "may return to office upon restoration of credibility and trust."

A 1975 survey in five North American Mennonite denominations found 60 percent of the respondents agreeing that the "churches should practice a thorough church discipline so that faltering members can be built up and restored or, in exceptional cases, excluded." Yet 35 percent of the same respondents agreed that "the way to work with members in the church who have lapsed from the standards of the church is never to exclude them from the church but rather to keep them on the membership roll, hoping they will mend their ways by heeding the advice of the minister or following the example of upright members."[18]

Some of the churches most interested as well as some least interested in church discipline today are large independent evangelical or fundamentalist churches. Some of these churches were formed in part to recover discipline. But by now many of them look much like the churches they left several decades ago, as an impartial observer will agree.

In many cases they are not well equipped to engage in discipline, mainly because they do not have a standing policy for it. They asserted their independence and withdrew from major denominations during the modernist-fundamentalist controversy, sometimes flouting the disciplines of these denominations in the process. Now they find this spirit of independence coming home to roost.

Many of these independent churches soon bump into the need for discipline. However, they must start from scratch because they do not bring with them the experience and traditions of discipline of their parent denominations. Such congregations may plead that they have the Bible as their guide for faith and practice. However, their search for a list of useful texts will not make up for the benefit of a history of theological reflection and ecclesiastical experience.

Large independent churches may also be handicapped in discipline precisely because they are independent. Independence may appear to promise freedom to discipline within the congregation, but the decisions reached will carry no authority beyond the congregation. There is no weight of denominational authority to back up the local congregation. Thus an individual under discipline can simply trot across the street to another independent church, which may not pay attention to appeals from the first congregation.

New England Congregationalists were certainly jealous for congregational polity. Even they urged that where needed, a "consociation of Churches should be used, as occasion doth require" for discipline problems extending beyond one congregation.[19]

It is somewhat curious that one pastor who argues for the "autonomous character" of "local churches" provides a good illustration of the problem of "church hoppers."

> I recall telephoning a neighboring pastor once after a couple who refused discipline joined his church. I . . . assured him I had no personal animosity toward them. I only wanted to spare him the heartache we had experienced, He reacted quite indifferently and that was the last I heard from him for over a year.

> Then word reached us that his church had split and he was no longer its pastor. I met this good brother a few months later and he said, "I wish I had listened to you. I didn't think you knew what you were talking about, that you were only bitter because you had lost these attractive folks to our church. If I had only listened, we wouldn't be in the mess we are in today."[20]

When people under discipline transfer to other congregations, one should judiciously communicate with those other congregations to avoid grief and to hold impenitent offenders accountable.[21] There is no evading the truth, however. The problem of easy transfer is one of the costs of the independence and disunity of the church.

One theologian addressing this problem suggests that a second congregation uncritically receiving an individual put out of the first should be itself declared "no church"—"as heathens and publicans."[22] Such an action is unrealistic and goes too far in declaring Christians of that congregation unfaithful without the due process of discipline.

If the above is the situation of many megachurches, it is even more the problem of parachurch organizations. There church discipline is often nonexistent. The organization, while claiming to be Christian, can also claim it is not a church. They want it both ways. Leaders who have built religious (and financial) empires are protected because of their "personality cult." Many people in the parachurch organizations are largely immune to discipline, though not necessarily to scandal or lawsuits. This is true because parachurch organizations are not accountable to a larger body such as a denomination. This actually may hold for many megachurches as well.

Concerning such situations one can only suggest that conscientious Christians must nonetheless address these people with the word of Christ. Christ's word and spirit are still the most effective instruments of both God's judgment and God's grace.

The contemporary scene should soon persuade us that a healthy future for the church will require the recovery of a faithful ministry of discipling.

10

THE VISIBLE CHURCH

The way to separate wheat from weeds
is not the way of violent eradication of the unrighteous.
It is the way of harvest,
the old God-ordained and time-honored way
of gathering people through the gospel.

Many people believe that the church discipline ideal proposed in this book can never become a reality because of the invisibility of the church. We have all heard some form of the claim that only God can tell saints from sinners. We finite mortals do not know who the elect are.

This problem seems even bigger if, as argued in the foregoing pages, the basis of discipline is not a legal code but spiritual life. One can identify acts of transgression, but isn't it presumptuous to claim to read people's hearts? The true church is invisible, runs the argument, and does not coincide with the visible organized church on earth.

It is not hard to see that this line of thought might decisively affect the conduct of discipline. At most one could admonish someone who *seems* to be in spiritual danger, according to our careful judgment. Even such an admonition might be completely unwarranted if we can't really read someone's spiritual condition. Certainly no church decision can be eternally valid. One might excommunicate a person whom God has not excommunicated or, on the other hand, forgive a person whom God has not forgiven.

Of course, this line of thought also calls into question the validity of baptism—even the existence of the church itself. If we cannot tell who is a true Christian for purposes of discipline, we can't tell in evangelism and baptism either. The logical consequence of the claim that the church is invisible is that we don't know whether our baptisms carry any spiritual significance. The whole enterprise of building the church is then a guessing game.

However, we do baptize people into the membership of the church. We do this, we believe, on the basis of recognizable faith. Practically all churches hold that life in Christ is the condition of membership in the church. If this is true, then taking people into membership signifies that we consider such life in Christ discernible.

Biblical and historic Christianity have operated under the conviction that membership in a visible church is of saving significance. If this is so, what is needed is a clarification of this underlying conviction and its application to the problem of discipline.

An adequate discussion of this problem must deal with the biblical passage which people have used more than any other to call church discipline into question. Time and again writers find in the parables of the wheat and the weeds (Matt. 13:24-30, 36-43) and of the fishnet (Matt. 13:47-50) scriptural and dominical authority for questioning the practice of discipline. Some even find grounds for invalidating altogether some aspects of discipline such as excommunication.

Tolerating Hypocrites

The interpretation of the parable of the weeds that has most highly influenced modern Protestantism comes from John Calvin:

> In my opinion, the design of the parable is simply this: so long as the pilgrimage of the Church in the world continues, bad

men and hypocrites will mingle in it with the good and upright, that the children of God may be armed with patience, and in the midst of offenses fitted to disturb them may preserve stead-fast faith.[1]

The most important thing to note in Calvin's interpretation of this parable is the application to the church.

When one applies the parable to the church, it contradicts the church's mandate to exercise discipline. A modern scholar following this line of thought is Joachim Jeremias. In a book on the parables he says:

> Men cannot discern the heart; if they attempt to make an effec-tive separation, they will inevitably commit errors of judgment and root up good wheat with the tares. Secondly, and more im-portant, God has fixed the moment of separation. The measure of time assigned by him must be fulfilled (Matt. 13:47). . . . The seed must be allowed to ripen. Then comes the harvest and with it the separation between the tares and wheat. . . . But that moment has not yet arrived. . . . Till then, all false zeal must be checked, the field must be left to ripen in patience . . . and everything left to God in faith, until his hour comes.[2]

According to this reading one *cannot* judge and one *must not* judge. One *cannot* because it is not possible for human eyes to distinguish the righteous from the unrighteous. One *must not* judge because it is not yet the time and also because it is not a human prerogative to do so. God will judge in God's own time and in God's own way through the "angels."

This interpretation throws the parable of the wheat and weeds into contradiction with the clear injunction to practice discipline in Matthew 18. It also contradicts the clear practice of discipline in the apostolic church (e.g., 1 Cor. 5).[3] Did Paul in 1 Corinthians 5 become impatient and judge before the time? More seriously, did Jesus contradict himself on this point? One writer accurately poses the problem: "Here the servants are forbidden to weed and bind, while later [in Matthew 16 and 18] the disciples are allowed [and even commanded] to bind."[4]

Many writers seem disturbed by this apparent contradiction and feel obliged to resolve it. Explanations have explored several approaches. One approach is frankly to admit a contradiction and to allow one of the opposing points of view to cancel the other. Thus, one writer points to Jesus' own nonjudgmental attitude (in John 8:1-11 and with Judas). He then argues that the few New Testament passages that support firm church discipline cannot stand in the way of the prevailing spirit of unfailing mercy in the New Testament. According to this writer the parable at least rules out all excommunication.[5]

An alternative approach has been to permit the parable to apply to only certain sins. Thus love must excuse fleshly weaknesses, but need not excuse false teaching and coarse sins, thought Zwingli.[6] Or the church is to tolerate only hypocrites, or those whose conversion is not hopeless. It need not tolerate manifest and obstinate offenders, says another writer.[7] Still another proposes that one should root out only heresy and scandal.[8] There is, however, no basis in this text for such discriminations.

Elementary reflection shows that the traditional problem of reconciling the parable with church discipline arises from a fundamentally faulty interpretation. The parable does not imply that one cannot distinguish saints from sinners. The very meaning of the entire parable rests on the assumption that they clearly can be distinguished. In the parable the servants point out to the householder something expressly forced upon their attention. There, before their eyes, stand identifiable weeds in a field of wheat.

The problem is not, then, inability to recognize the weeds, because recognizing them only too well is what raises the problem. The central question in the parable, which even a superficial reading shows, is what to do with this existing, highly visible problem. That is, in view of an obviously weedy field, how can one achieve the necessary and even inevitable separation?

Archibald Hunter suggests that this parable "sounds like Jesus' reply to a critic—probably a Pharisee (the very name meant 'separatist') who had objected: 'If the Kingdom of God is really here, why has there not been a separating of sinners from saints in Israel?' "[9] Jeremias writes in a similar vein: "Everywhere in the time of Jesus we meet with attempts to set up the Messianic community.... The Pharisees clearly claimed to represent the holy community."[10]

Some Jewish authorities definitely wanted to weed out sinners, as we can see from the story about the woman taken in adultery recorded in John 8:1-11. Others like Simon the Zealot or James and John (in Luke 9:54) "with an irreligious solicitude for God ... wanted to accelerate the kingdom's advance by direct action."[11] They sought to achieve the reign of God through violence and terrorism. The Pharisees sought to impose it with "law and order." To all such approaches Jesus gave his decisive answer. One cannot establish the kingdom of God by violent eradication of the unrighteous.

Gathering the Harvest

Does Jesus' rejection of the violent and coercive methods advocated by others mean that a weedy field must be tolerated? Does this mean that a righteous community cannot be realized until the end of the world? Many interpreters go astray at this point because they identify the harvest here ("the close of the age") as the final judgment at the end of present history.

However, Jesus considers his own coming to be the close of the old age and the advent of the new. The harvest is therefore a process going on in his own ministry. As C. H. Dodd says, "It does not seem necessary to suppose that the judgment is treated as a new event in the future." This is true because "the coming of the kingdom of God is in the teaching of Jesus not a momentary event but a complex of interrelated events including his own ministry, his death, and what follows, all conceived as forming a unity.''[12] Although the opening verses of Matthew 13 liken the proclamation of the kingdom to sowing, other passages illustrate the coming of the kingdom as a harvest.

> The Johannine equivalent for the synoptic saying, "The harvest truly is plenteous," is to be found in the words, "Lift up your eyes and behold the fields, that they are white unto harvest" (John 4:35). The whole context reads as follows: "Do not say, 'Four whole months yet, and the harvest comes.' Behold I say to you, lift up your eyes and observe the fields, that they are white for harvest. Already the reaper is taking his pay, and gathering a crop for eternal life, so that the sower and reaper may rejoice together. For in this the saying is true: 'One sows and another reaps.' I sent you to reap that on which you have not laboured. Others have entered into their labour.''[13]

From the foregoing observations it is clear that the parable of the wheat and the weeds means almost the opposite of what many take it to mean. Jesus does not reject the attempt to establish a pure community. Instead, he points out the only effective way to establish such a community.

There is an effective way of separating wheat from weeds, a way of establishing a separated, righteous community which embodies the rule of God. But it is not the way of violent eradication of the unrighteous. It is the way of harvest, the old God-ordained and time-honored way of gathering people through gospel proclamation. If the seed that has been sown is left to do its work, it will come to fruition in God's time and way. Jesus warns his followers that the only legitimate and possible way of establishing the reign of God is to proclaim the Word, gather the righteous, and leave the wicked to the divine wrath.

This is the only logical interpretation of this parable. For if there is no separation till the future judgment, then there can also be no gathering of the harvest, no missionary reaping, no church. However, there *was* a great commission given, and a church does exist in the world. It stands as a witness to the separating work of the gospel of the kingdom.

Most commentators consider the parable of the net (Matt. 13:47-50) a parallel to the parable of the wheat and the weeds. Jeremias says,

> Both parables . . . are concerned with the final judgment which ushers in the kingdom of God; it is compared to a separation. [However,] God has fixed the moment of separation. The measure of time assigned by him must be fulfilled . . . but that moment has not yet arrived.[14]

This interpretation leaves incomprehensible the statement in the parable that it is the fishermen themselves who sort out the fish.

C. H. Dodd gives a much more natural and coherent interpretation of this parable.

> Now the point of the story is that when you are fishing with a dragnet you cannot expect to select your fish: your catch will be a mixed one. . . . But—there is after all a process of selection; . . . there is a sifting of possible followers of Jesus. . . . Here then we have an interpretation of the parable which brings it into line with the other saying of Jesus, and relates it to the actual course of his ministry. The kingdom of God, in process of realization in and through that ministry, is like the work of fishing with a drag-net, for the appeal is made to all indiscriminately, and yet in the nature of things it is selective; and, let us recall, this selection *is* the divine judgment, though men pass it upon themselves by sheer ultimate attitude to the appeal.[15]

We can now draw our conclusions about the teaching of these parables and their bearing upon church discipline. They do bear on discipline indirectly, since the parables are concerned primarily with the calling out of a righteous community through missionary proclamation. However, these parables do not discourage the practice of discipline. They in fact teach how the church should carry on its discipling ministry—by the use of the Word of the gospel, not by violence.

Rudolf Bohren is one of the few scholars who discerns the correct meaning of the parable of the wheat and weeds and hence its bearing upon the subject of church discipline.

> The parable and the explanation discuss the relation of the disciples to the surrounding world, not, however, the relation of the disciples with each other. . . . Church discipline shall not become world discipline. Jesus then did not fight against church discipline. One may not play off the parable of the weeds against church discipline.[16]

That expresses it: "Church discipline shall not become world discipline." The church should not try to impose its discipline upon the world, and its discipline should not be worldly in nature. Expressed in positive terms, church discipline should disciple only the church—and do so in keeping with the church's norms.

Ironically, those in church history who were most eloquent in their appeal to the parable of the weeds were the very ones who did not heed its true message. Augustine appealed to the parable in his controversy with the Donatists, arguing for Catholic tolerance against the Donatist demand for stricter separation of the righteous. But then he endorsed the suppression of the Donatist heresy by imperial force.[17]

Calvin pleaded for tolerance in the name of the parable. But he insisted upon uprooting one particularly obnoxious weed—Michael Servetus—that seemed to stand in the way of his establishing God's kingdom in Geneva. He had Michael Servetus burned at the stake.

One of Calvin's contemporaries, Menno Simons, was aware of the real meaning of the parable. With a price of one hundred gulden on his head, he happened to be one of the weeds the Catholic Church was trying to uproot. Perhaps Menno learned the meaning of the parable from personal experience.[18]

Martin Luther also interpreted the parable rightly.

> In this parable the field is the world. The wheat means the good children and the tares the bad.... We are not to be affrighted by this because the devil is always among the children of God. As for the treatment of these heretics, we are here told that we are not to exterminate them, since he who errs today may turn to the right course tomorrow. Who knows if the Word of God will touch his heart? But if he is burned or strangled, he is prevented from coming to the truth and thus he is lost who might have been saved. The Lord points out furthermore the danger that the wheat will be destroyed along with the tares. See, then, how frightful we have been that for so long we have handled the Turks with the sword, heretics with fire, and have sought by killing to force the Jews to the faith, to root out the tares by our own power, as if we were the people to rule over hearts and spirits. I would rather tolerate an entire unchristian land for the sake of one Christian in the midst than to exterminate one Christian with the unchristians.[19]

Doubtless the main reason for the abuse of the parable in the long history of Christendom is that many identified the field with the church. They held this interpretation even though Matthew says that the field is the world. This is partly understandable, since the church was for most of the Constantinian era identified with the European world.

Nevertheless, *church* and *world* are the distinction under which alone the church can obey the teaching of the parable. Only by recognizing this distinction can the gospel of the kingdom establish and maintain a separated and righteous community of faith.

Confusing the church and the world while postulating an invisible church usually leads to one or more deplorable consequences. Sometimes the church expects the secular authorities to relieve it of the responsibility of discipline. This was, unfortunately, too common in the state churches of Protestantism, as noted earlier. Sometimes the church tries to divide legal responsibilities between itself and the secular order. This allows it to classify sins, dealing with supposedly religious ones itself (e.g., sexual morals) while leaving so-called civil matters to the state (e.g., business ethics). Sometimes the church in its discipline reverts to the secular world's methods of criminal law.

The answer to all these confusions is the recognition of a visible church and its distinction from the world. Then the church is able to go about its task of discipline in the same way it goes about evangelism—according to norms derived from the gospel. The other option—postulating an invisible church—almost invariably leads the church to confuse its discipline with secular law.

A Visible Church

The parable of the wheat and the weeds would not have been such a problem in the church's history if the invisible church idea had not been read into it. The Swiss theologian Emil Brunner claims that this doctrine came into Western theology through Augustine.

Augustine's study taught him that the church of the New Testament was quite different from what he saw around him in the institutional church of his own times. Since both were called the church, Augustine used the terms *invisible church* and *visible church* to distinguish them. According to Brunner, the Reformers Zwingli and Calvin "took over this fundamental concept." However, Brunner goes on to say, this concept of an invisible church "is wholly foreign to the New Testament."[20]

It should not be hard to see that the term *invisible church* is an anomaly. It does not really mean one cannot tell who is a true Christian. For the distinction between the visible church and the invisible church rests upon the observation that not everyone in a given institutional church is a true believer. If this were not obviously and patently visible, the distinction would be quite unnecessary. If the invisible church really were invisible, one would have no reason for positing it over against the visible church.

The real problem in church discipline is not the supposed inability to discern the true saints. The problem is what to do about the contradiction between the New Testament norm and an existing situation. The issue is not the discernment of the faithful but of what to do about the faithless.

The position taken here on the visibility of the church and the discipline it entails does not necessarily presuppose believers (or adult) baptism. For pedobaptist churches also seek to define their membership by faith. To achieve or even retain full membership, persons baptized as children should later be confirmed. That is, they should themselves evince living faith.

In principle the major Reformers opposed a system of levels of membership such as existed in distinctions between monks or clergy and laity. They claimed that one faith was to be the constitutive basis of the church. Reformation theology does not warrant the two levels of membership often freely admitted and even justified and encouraged by the doctrine of an invisible church.

Our contention that the church is visible does not mean one can predict who will become saints in the future—that is, who will ultimately be numbered among the elect. The boundaries of the church are continuously changing. No one can expect to divine or control where these boundaries will finally lie.

Nevertheless, God has called out the church and set it in the midst of the world to proclaim the gospel. It must acknowledge and endorse where people's response to the gospel sets the boundaries of the church from time to time. And it can assert that these boundaries are of saving significance.

Furthermore, the claim made here for the visibility of the church does not mean a Christian can immediately recognize saints at any time and at any place on earth. It does not even suggest that the church will always avoid error despite careful observation. It does mean, however, that the true Christian disciple is soon recognizable and that questionable cases are subject to investigation and correction.

No sophistry refutes this point. True, a woman may not be able to recognize her own sister under certain circumstances (e.g., 29½ minutes after sunset at 333 feet in a slight rain). This does not mean she cannot confidently identify her under average circumstances. The question is whether and how she will investigate if the person in question really is her sister.

Here the illustration becomes a parable. Wherever there may be doubt, concerned Christians will try to make sure about the faith of others. People of faith also seek to make themselves known to others. This conviction lay at the heart of the "watch and care" of early Methodism. Wesley said:

> I had been often told it was impossible for me to distinguish the precious from the vile without the miraculous discernment of spirits. But I now saw, more clearly than ever, that this might be done ... without much difficulty, supposing only two things; first courage and steadiness in the examiner; secondly, common sense and common honesty in the leader of each class.... The question is not concerning the heart, but the life.... The general tenor of this I do not say cannot be known, but cannot be hid without a miracle.[21]

One might still rightly reply, "There is always a margin of church members over whom there is some question." Granted there are those, on the one hand, who show no fruit of the Spirit in their lives nor any marks of repentance. On the other hand, there are those whose life leaves no doubt about their discipleship. Neither of these groups represents a problem. The problem supposedly arises with those in the church whose conduct is in the in-between "gray area."

One of the functions of church discipline is to deal precisely with this problem area, this margin on the boundary of the church. Discipline admits uncertainty about these people. What should one do about church members whose spiritual status comes into question? The "invisible church" position discourages action about them. The consequence of this view is neglect of discipline.

We claim that the margin over which there is question—the hazy boundary between obvious saints and obvious sinners—is actually an argument *for* discipline instead of against it. If faith should be openly confessed, and if the faith of some comes into question, the situation calls for inquiry. That is, if the church is in doubt about certain persons, it should invite them to make their Christian confession and conduct unambiguously clear. If they do not, the church must, in love, warn them that they are deceiving themselves about their salvation. Otherwise, responsible people in the church are failing to define the meaning of discipleship and are contributing to people's self-deception.

As this book has asserted repeatedly, discipline begins with concern for people whose spiritual condition stands in uncertainty. Discipline does not expect to finish its task by producing an absolutely "pure church." Such a static church with a finally fixed and unchanging boundary would not be a living church. A living and healthy church is one that is faithful in the ongoing mission of making disciples, thereby expanding the boundaries of the church.

Where the church is not faithfully narrowing the margin over which there is uncertainty, a backlog builds up and the margin grows. It must then return to the task of evangelism. This, as we have seen, is once more the task of discipling people. The church cannot escape its responsibility to bring people into the way of Christ, both without the church and within it.

11

THE RULE OF CHRIST

The rule of Christ means doing something
about sin in the church—
but doing it Christ's way.

One of the ever-present points of controversy in the history of church discipline has been the nature of the church's authority to forgive. Matthew 18:18-20 says:

> Truly, I say to you, whatever you bind on earth shall be bound in heaven, and whatever you loose on earth shall be loosed in heaven. Again I say to you, if two of you agree on earth about anything they ask, it will be done for them by my Father in heaven. For where two or three are gathered in my name, there am I in the midst of them.

Here, as in John 20:22-23 and Matthew 16:15-18, God in some sense gives the church the authority to loose or bind, to remit or retain, to forgive or withhold forgiveness of sin. Now, to many the church's claim to have this authority sounds presumptuous, because the church thereby pretends to usurp the prerogative of God's authority to forgive sin.

Authority Is Not Autonomy

The church's authority to bind and loose in discipline is

sometimes considered the natural right usually thought to belong to any human organization. One writer states:

> It belongs to the very nature of a society, and is inherent therein, the power to admit to membership those who profess to act in accordance with its rules, and to exclude those who violate the conditions on which they were admitted. By the nature of its constitutions, as well as in virtue of certain privileges granted by its founder, the church is vested with a similar power.[1]

Another says, "Every institution that has the right to make laws also possesses the right to punish transgressors of these laws."[2]

Church discipline, however, goes beyond the rights of an independent human organization. Church discipline

> must be distinguished from all disciplines and jurisdictions based on human rights. In this sense every human organization protects itself in some fashion or other by a kind of discipline of its members—every union, party, corporation (. . . for example, a university), every political association, every military organization, and every state. . . . Now church discipline is often enough misunderstood and misrepresented in this way. . . . Church discipline is not, however, exercised in the name of human justice but through an authority delegated to the church by Christ.[3]

In discipline we are not, therefore, dealing with the self-government of an institution. Discipline presupposes subjection of the church to the rule of Christ. Strictly speaking, the church can only be an instrument of the authority of its Lord. That is the presupposition for saying that what is done on earth is done also in heaven.

Asserting church autonomy instead of accepting Christ's authority is unfortunately a widespread error. People speak of "our church" and "your church" as though it belongs to them, not to God. They assume denominations or conferences have the right to set rules and conditions of membership for themselves, forgetting that God sets the conditions of membership in God's church. The church's responsibility is to observe the will of its Lord.

What then is the right relationship between God and the church in the authority to exercise discipline? An answer to this must begin by clearing away some popular but mistaken notions.

Authority Is Not Ratification

The first mistaken notion is that God has committed himself to ratify the decisions of the church. By delegating to the church the power of absolution, goes this line of thought, God has bound himself to endorse in heaven what the church decides upon earth. As one writer expresses it, "Whatever sentence shall be passed and declared by the Governors of the church shall be ratified by Christ whom they represent: which is no more than may be said of the vicegerent of any other prince."[4]

But God does not simply ratify every decision in binding and loosing, as though he has become a prisoner of the church's will. As one theologian says, "In spite of its being delegated, the authority of church discipline does not cease to remain Christ's authority. It can therefore be exercised only in his name and according to his will."[5] Unfortunately, this implies the possibility of a discipline not exercised according to Christ's will.

Is this not a fateful admission that calls into serious question all church discipline? Not necessarily. First, while discipline involves the church in commitment to decisions, these are not arbitrary decisions. They are attempts by the church to be the executive agency of divine decisions. Second, these decisions are not hidden in inaccessible divine mystery but made known to the church through God's Word and Holy Spirit. Moreover, the church's reading of such decisions is always subject to review and amendment.

These principles governing the nature of the authority of the church are a warning to the church that it must take its guidance from the Word and Holy Spirit in making its decisions. They also buttress its real and legitimate authority when it does so. In other words, discipline must be based on the gospel, on Christ's requirements for discipleship.

When the church usurps the authority of Christ it merely replaces the requirement of faith with its own doctrine and standards such as eating fish on Friday or forbidding the use of buttons. A church that does this sooner or later undermines its authority, for people eventually recognize this to be a human imposition, not the authority of Christ through his church.

Recognizing the weakness of the view that God ratifies the decisions of the church has led some to attempt to reverse the picture. These persons say that the church must ratify God's decisions instead. Thus one writer argues:

> Over half of Christendom believes in sacerdotalism, that is, that certain men have been divinely authorized to forgive sins in behalf of God. And the above passages [John 20:23; Matt. 16:19; 18:18] are the ones quoted to substantiate such a doctrine. My thesis is to prove that the perfect tense has been mistranslated in these passages, and consequently ... there is no basis for sacerdotalism or priestly absolution in the New Testament.[6]

The writer just cited contends that one should translate the texts noted, "Whatsoever is bound on earth shall have been bound in heaven, and whatsoever is loosed on earth shall have been loosed in heaven." Accordingly, "Jesus warned the disciples that they were to treat as forgiven only those that were already forgiven by God."[7]

The question of "priestly absolution" aside, this interpretation does not hold up exegetically. It falls into contradiction with a text such as Mark 2:5 and its parallel, Luke 5:20. There the same form of expression is used to describe Jesus' forgiveness of the paralytic. As one commentator says, "Luke, like those bystanders, thought that Jesus claimed to forgive sins, not that he treated 'as forgiven only those that were already forgiven by God.' "[8] In this incident God's forgiveness and Jesus' forgiveness of the paralytic are not two separate actions. They are one action, Jesus being the instrument of God's gracious forgiveness. In the words of Jesus, "The Son of man has authority on earth to forgive sins."

For this reason the church has often taken this story as a model of its authority to forgive sin. "The complete identification of the church's and God's judgment is here brought out in its full force. In the church God's judgment is not merely proclaimed, but realized. The church's action is the action of God's presence itself."[9]

The church's decisions in binding and loosing are therefore not just echoes of an action completed by God and then parroted by the church. Rather, the church is involved in the process, united with God as an instrument of his saving work. This point is clear also in other aspects of the texts on binding and loosing. In Matthew 16:18 the promise, "I will give you the keys of the kingdom of heaven," is tied to Jesus' declaration, "On this rock I will build my church."

In Matthew 18:19 Jesus promises, "If two of you agree on earth about anything they ask, it will be done for them." This promise in turn rests upon another: "For where two or three are gathered in my name, there am I in the midst of them."

In John 20:23 we read, "If you forgive the sins of any, they are forgiven; if you retain the sins of any, they are retained." Again, this promise is based on the words, "As the Father has sent me, even so I send you. . . . Receive the Holy Spirit."

Authority Is Not Two Churches

The idea that God ratifies the decisions of the church or that the church ratifies the decisions of God is no longer widespread today. More common is the notion that no connection necessarily exists between these respective decisions. This notion usually depends on the distinction between the visible and invisible churches. The visible church is held to be the the human organization on earth; the invisible church, the heavenly number of the elect.

This view essentially denies that what is bound or loosed on earth is bound or loosed in heaven. It holds that any action the church takes can affect only a person's standing in the human institution. It does not necessarily touch an individual's status before God. Between the visible church and the invisible church there is no certain connection.

Making the authority of God and that of the church two separate, unrelated realms avoids the blasphemous claim that God is trapped by his own promise of Matthew 18:18 and that ecclesiastical institutions control the gates of heaven. However, the net effect of this position is to void the significance of the church's decisions.

The church does not try to dissociate itself from God's action in baptism. There it addresses specific individuals in Christ's name and requires a specific response. Baptism is the enacted Word, the Word's effective operation. Baptism is a sacrament in the proper sense of that term, "the sign *and* the thing signified." The sign effects what it signifies. Thus the minister says to the candidate, "I baptize you in the name of the Father, Son, and Holy Spirit," rightly assuming to be the effective agent of God's working.

The same principle holds in discipline. If discipline is a function of the gospel, then absolution or excommunication are necessary responses to people's reception or rejection of the gospel. They are the enactment of the forgiving or hardening effects of the Word. The decision of discipline in absolution or excommunication is no different from that made in baptism. It is the very activity of God in and through the church.

Authority Only to Forgive?

There are those who seem bothered by the thought that the church would presume to exclude people from the kingdom of God. These persons seem quite untroubled, however, by the thought that the church presumes to *include* people as it does in baptism. Furthermore, every act of inclusion itself already implies an exclusion: the exclusion of those not included! One scholar in discussing the authority to bind and loose says,

> Doubtless we must follow some rough criteria in distinguishing among those who claim to be followers of Christ. But I would much prefer to err on the side of recognizing some whom God does not recognize than excluding those whom he has accepted as his own. [10]

We could as logically say, Why not be strict and let God be gracious in the end? Would that not be better than pretending to be more charitable than God and in the process offering false comfort to people about a matter of momentous importance?

We need not be either more generous or more strict than God, because we have more than "rough criteria." As the scholar just quoted goes on to say, the "canonical limits" of the church "should extend to the charismatic limits."

> Those who call upon the name of the Lord in faith, who are baptized in his name, have received the Spirit which he gives, and look forward to the consummation of his kingdom—these belong to his body and are the people whom God has called for himself. . . .
>
> Wherever the saving grace of God is found, there is the Church. [11]

Exactly. The corollary is that the church must warn those who reject God's saving grace. If they remain impenitent, it must exclude those still claiming membership in God's church.

Interestingly, the modern tendency to accept the church's authority to forgive but not its authority to excommunicate is just the opposite of the ancient church's tendency. Like Tertullian, the church held that it can excommunicate but not forgive. Tertullian, as we have noticed, was effectively answered by the Catholic Church. It said that binding and loosing are parallel, as shown in the church's practice of discriminating baptism, which all had to recognize was the exercise of this dual authority.

Let those with an inclination toward lenience note that in Matthew 18 the prescription for discipline ends with the individual a "Gentile and tax collector." And the parable of the unforgiving servant ends with him in prison because of his abuse of the forgiveness of the king. Of course, excommunication need not be the last word for anyone. As we have insisted earlier, excommunication does not close the door of the church against an offender's return. Instead, it means that an offender is not in a state of grace until he or she returns. Meanwhile, the most promising way of encouraging an offender's return is faithfulness to the gospel. Its principle of judgment is consistent with its basic theme of love.

Judge Not That You Be Not Judged

One text often invoked to forbid or discourage discipline is the word of Jesus in the Sermon on the Mount, Matthew 7:1-5.

> Judge not, that you be not judged. For with the judgment you pronounce you will be judged, and the measure you give will be the measure you get. Why do you see the speck that is in your brother's eye, but do not notice the log that is in your own eye? . . . You hypocrite, first take the log out of your own eye, and then you will see clearly to take the speck out of your brother's eye.

A little examination will show that this word of Jesus is no excuse for neglecting church discipline. In the first place, judgment is exactly what Jesus engages in here. He is admonishing and correcting his disciples. Second, Jesus states that we will be judged as we judge. If then our judgment is to help our neighbor with compassion rather than to condemn, we may expect compassionate help and not condemnation ourselves. Third, Jesus invites his hearers to take the log out of their own eye in order to be able to remove the speck from their brother's eye. One is not to keep one's log and enjoy it as an excuse for neglecting to help someone else! This word of Jesus does not then discourage discipling. Rather, it encourages and exemplifies the *right way* of discipling people. It does not contravene the counsel of Matthew 18.

The persons most ready to invoke the words of Jesus in Matthew 7 about not judging are often the ones most ready to engage in judgment in secular life. Few besides confirmed anarchists would hesitate to endorse the act of judgment when it comes to arson, burglary, assault, drunken driving, or business fraud. This shows that it is not a question of *whether* we will judge but only of *what* we will judge and *how*.

Concerning *what* we will judge, the question is whether secular society or Christian norms will decide our standards. On *how* we will judge, the question is whether we will judge punitively, as the state, or redemptively, as taught by Christ.

Authority Is Ministry

The church cannot avoid judging. It will recognize respective responses to its proclamation of the gospel, in baptizing or refusing to baptize, forgiving or recognizing impenitence. How can the church preach that the unrighteous will not inherit the kingdom of God (1 Cor. 6:9) and yet pretend that it cannot make a decision when confronted by unrighteousness? It is indeed God who excludes, but God works through the church. Restricting the meaning of binding and loosing to general absolution, as in the Sunday morning liturgy, is an unjustified limitation of its meaning.[12]

The key consideration in discipline is an individual's response to the word of the gospel. Nevertheless, the church cannot avoid its responsibility in recognizing responses. It will plead for a decision of faith. But if that is not forthcoming, it will reluctantly acknowledge the decision of unfaith. This process is simply what we mean by discipline.

Some fear that discipline will presume to be more than the effectual declaration of God's Word. Simply because it has so presumed in much of ecclesiastical history, we must not make it less. That is, the church cannot decline to exclude impenitent persons from the kingdom of Christ, for that would be the surest way of actually excluding them. For by not making known the truth, the church would confirm such persons in their complacency and self-deception.

Lesslie Newbigin makes a helpful statement on the point under discussion in a comment upon 1 Corinthians 5.

> When Paul writes . . . [about] the excommunication of the erring brother, it is very clear that he does not say or imply that it is simply a matter of the sinner cutting himself off. He calls for a very solemn and deliberate act of the fellowship—an act in which he himself is completely associated. Moreover, this act is not regarded as merely a severance of external membership, while leaving the man's spiritual relationship with Christ untouched. . . . To be in the Church's fellowship was to be in Christ, and to be cast out of it was to be delivered over to Satan.[13]

Similarly, another theologian, writing out of the missionary situation, maintains that the church's proclamation and warning

> do not come only in the form of general statements. It is the duty of those responsible in the church to address them quite specifically to persons who are plainly living heedless of the claim of Christ. . . . We recognize a solemn authority which the

Lord has given to his church actually to exclude from its fellow-ship any who refuse its warning. Where this authority is reverently exercised in obedience to the Lord's own will . . . the decisions so taken are not of merely earthly significance but concern the eternal destiny of the person concerned.[14]

Max Thurian sums up the nature of the church's authority in discipline in his words on John 20:23.

This ministry is an aspect of the power of the keys, which ought to be understood as including the whole of the Church's task of setting men free. . . . It is not a question of the ministry of preaching only but of a word and an act which operate what they signify. . . . The Church believes that God acts conjointly and effectually in a sign which she addresses to the believers. [It is an] act which entails the action of God himself.[15]

The Rule of Christ

A familiar expression at the time of the Reformation was the phrase "the rule of Christ." Any religiously informed person who heard it recognized it as virtually a code word for Matthew 18:15-20. This expression was still common among English Baptists in the 1600s and Baptists in the Southern U.S. in the Pre-Civil War 1800s. They used it to designate what Christ taught in Matthew 18 about how to deal with sin in the church.

The phrase *rule of Christ* carried two implications. First, it protested the drunkenness, false oaths, violence, and debauchery too often tolerated in the church at the time. Second, it protested the church's use of the sword and stake to impose what it considered to be the authority of Christ in dealing with offenders. *The rule of Christ meant to do something about sin in the church but to do it Christ's way.*

The rule of Christ. That is finally the church's authority for discipling wayward believers. Christ's example and spirit are the church's inspiration. The church must not abandon the erring. Rather, it must persistently invite them to return to the way of Christ. Christ's instruction is the church's guide for how to go about this task. The way Christ reached out to sinners, restored them, and made them his disciples remains our model for church discipline.

Appendix

QUESTIONS FOR REFLECTION AND DISCUSSION

Chapter 1: The Mandate for Discipling

1. What do Jesus' sayings about the keys of the kingdom mean? See Matthew 18:15-18.

2. What is the nature of the reign of God in the church?

3. In what sense is the establishment of the kingdom an act of God and in what sense does it depend upon the work of believers?

4. Evaluate the suggestion that missionary proclamation and admonition of fellow believers are both acts of discipling.

5. How does the task of discipling relate to evangelism?

6. Is there one basis for getting rightly related to God and a second, different one for good standing in the church? (See pages [30, 31].) What view of the church lies behind the distinction mentioned on page [31]?

7. The subject of this book is emotionally loaded for some people. How do *you* feel about it? If necessary, reread this first important chapter.

Chapter 2: The Occasion for Discipling

1. As pointed out in chapter 2, many Christians are confused

about when one should go to one's sister or brother. What sins call for discipline?

2. When should we evangelize? When should we baptize? Do the answers to these questions suggest when we should go to someone with concerns about his or her spiritual health or life?

3. Is it possible for someone to harbor secret sin indefinitely? Is something wrong with a congregation that can see only acts, but cannot discern a spiritual state?

4. What does a healthy spiritual life look like? How can you tell whether someone has spiritual life? Do you need biblical criteria? Do you need to have spiritual life to recognize it in someone else? (In other words, does it take one to know one?)

5. Are private sins less harmful than public ones?

6. Mention some of the danger signals that indicate loss of spiritual life and reversion to a state of sin. Do you tend to think of things like adultery, theft, and murder, or of things like loss of joy, love, kindness, and mercy?

7. Discuss "unforgivable sin" versus "unforgivable sinner" in relation to 1 John 5:16-18 and the discussion on pages [40-42]. Many Christians think there is such a thing as an unforgivable sin. Now and then some people tend to think they have committed it. What does the author say about this?

8. Does it make sense to think of sin and faith as opposites? Or sin and the Spirit of Christ? Is sin a state of being?

Chapter 3: The Method of Discipling

1. Who should go to the sister or brother? What is the proper procedure? Who should initiate the process of discipling?

2. How should we go? Are some approaches better than others?

3. How can one change the perceptions of the church on this subject? How can a fellowship achieve the frame of mind that giving and receiving counsel is normal—the accepted and expected thing?

4. Does your congregation have a policy on this matter? Is there an understanding between minister and congregation? How can a congregation ensure that cases don't "fall between the cracks"? What lines of communication and responsibility would be helpful?

5. Are honesty and love compatible? Can we respect the truth about someone's life and still show the love of Christ?

6. Sketch some hypothetical cases of discipling. Be as detailed as you wish. How much time is needed for admonition? How long should someone be given to come to a decision? How quickly can the church discern one's spiritual status? Is it reasonable to allow a case to continue in process one or more years?

Chapter 4: The Goal of Discipling

1. What are some misconceptions about forgiveness?

2. What is the real meaning of forgiveness?

3. How should forgiveness be applied in the process of discipling someone?

4. Some people think of forgiveness as the cancellation of charges or executive clemency. Chapter 4 calls forgiveness the recognition of beginning, renewed, or resumed life in the Spirit. What difference does this distinction make?

5. Who accepts the cost of forgiveness? Debate about the meaning of forgiveness has often separated the act of the forgiver *from* the responsibility of the sinner. The definition of forgiveness in this book would call *both* to action. The forgiver accepts responsibility to walk with the sinner in a new way of life, the life in the Spirit. But the sinner too accepts responsibility to open himself or herself to life in the Spirit.

6. Suppose a member of your church was charged with assault and battery and the story appeared in the community paper. Suggest what a Christian confession ought to involve if the individual genuinely repents.

7. Why are we able to rejoice at the conversion of a notorious

sinner, sometimes regarding that person as a "trophy of grace," but then feel embarrassed at such a confession by a church member?

8. How does a confession of faith differ from a criminal confession? How can we keep connotations of the latter out of church discipline? (See pages [69-71].) "The test of a sincere confession is not just the factual accuracy of a report of someone's past behavior. It is the evidence of a new lifestyle which shows that the person is leaving such behavior behind."

Chapter 5: Redemptive Excommunication

1. Is it harder to get into your church, or harder to get out? Why? How would this compare with the requirements of membership in secular organizations such as service clubs in your community?

2. How can excommunication ever possibly be redemptive? Is there anything Christian about kicking people out of the church?

3. What is excommunication? What message does the church want to give in excommunicating someone? What message do most people receive when someone is excommunicated? Is there a discrepancy here? What can be done about it?

4. Sometimes worried parents of grown children want the church to continue to carry their children's names on the roll, even though those children may be living like unbelievers in the next state. How do you feel about this? How should the church work at this issue?

5. What difference does it make to see excommunication as recognition of a fact rather than as sentencing of an offender?

6. Do you agree that spiritual life is an all-or-nothing proposition? Can one be half-baptized? Can one be half-excommunicated? What does this say about discipling as an ongoing, normal task in the church?

7. What about communion? If someone is not fit for communion, is that person fit to continue as a member of the

church? What are some of the possible implications of with-holding communion from a member?

Chapter 6: Avoidance and Restoration

1. What is the Christian meaning of avoidance?

2. In what specific ways is a Christian's relationship to a non-Christian different from his relationship to a fellow Christian?

3. Name some alternatives to Jesus' treatment of tax collectors that the church has sometimes practiced in history (e.g., flogging, imprisonment, economic sanctions, loss of civil rights, public humiliation [New England Puritans], etc.). Is this what Jesus meant for us to do?

4. How might a person earn Jesus' reputation: "He is a friend of tax collectors and sinners"? Sketch a modern-day version of this.

5. Do you understand the distinction between spiritual and natural social relationships discussed in connection with 1 Corinthians 7 on pages [98-99]? What adjustments would be appropriate in a young adult group in which one person lost his or her spiritual life and consequently membership in the church?

Chapter 7: Addressing the Task

1. How can a congregation carry out its responsibilities in the task of discipling a believer?

2. Discuss the author's comment, "Church discipline is of one piece with the church's preaching and living of the gospel in the world. Under no circumstances may we neglect the responsibility of reaching out with help to people in spiritual trouble."

3. Begin with a study of the meaning of Christian life. Is helping a fellow believer with her Christian life an act of caring or an invasion of privacy?

4. How can your congregation begin to take a different, more redemptive approach to persons needing discipline?

What are some of the first steps?

5. What would happen if your church took the next case of a need for discipling and carried it through with all the love, sensitivity, and honesty that it could?

6. What will it take for this to be more than an interesting and stimulating (but abstract and ultimately irrelevant) study? That is, what will it take to make the practice advocated by this book a reality in your congregation? Is your congregation ready to take the steps necessary to make it a reality?

Chapter 8: The Historical Record

1. Recall the overall sweep of God's dealings with humanity in the Bible and throughout history. What does it mean that God called out of this world for his purposes a people? How do we hold membership in this people of God?

2. What has been the church's record? Make a survey of this aspect of the church's life. Something can be learned from the church's failures as well as from its successes.

3. The church has, at least until recently, kept the practice of discipline. Why, then, has so little been written about the practice of discipline compared to our witness on peace, relief, nonconformity, and evangelism?

Chapter 9: The Contemporary Scene

1. What kind of discipling does your church presently practice? Is it consistent with the nature of the church as defined by Jesus in the New Testament?

2. What difference would it make for discipline to require living faith as a condition for membership in the church?

3. Find out what the church discipline policy of other denominations is. What can you learn from them both negatively and positively?

4. Procedures easily become formalized, routinized, and institutionalized in the church. One case sets a precedent, and then it becomes law. How can the church avoid this?

Chapter 10: The Visible Church

1. What is the fallacy of the argument some people make for an invisible church?

2. If a believers church calls for believers baptism, doesn't it also call for believers discipline? That is, if baptism should be correlated with the beginning of new life in Christ, shouldn't appropriate measures be taken where there is imminent or actual cessation of spiritual life?

3. When is the harvest of the wheat and the tares? Is it a future event or a present reality with the beginning of the reign of God in Christ? (See pages [157-158].)

4. What does church membership mean in your church?

5. What are some of the characteristics of the Christian life? (See, among other texts, Eph. 2, Col. 3, 1 Cor. 13, and Matt. 5—7.)

6. Is baptism in your church consciously based on recognition of the Spirit of Christ in the candidate for baptism? Or is it a puberty ceremony in which adolescents are coached to adopt respectable adult values?

7. Why did the apostolic church make a distinction between preaching and teaching? (Preaching meant proclamation of the good news to non-Christians who were without faith and spiritual life. Teaching was directed to Christians and presupposed spiritual life.)

Chapter 11: The Rule of Christ

1. Is judging always wrong? Compare Matthew 7:1 with 7:5-6. What makes judging wrong?

2. What is the task of an ambassador at a peace negotiation? Do ambassadors try to second-guess the position of their own government? Or are governments in such close touch with

their ambassadors that they can act through them? Does this analogy hold for the church?

3. What is the meaning of the words in the baptismal service, "I baptize you in the name of the Father and of the Son and of the Holy Spirit"? (See page [171].)

4. Does the church have the right to forgive a person's sins in the name of God? On what do you base your answer?

5. Does the church have the right to withhold forgiveness from a person in the name of God? (See pages [173-174].) On what do you base your answer?

6. What is the relationship of authority and ministry? (See pages [174-176].)

7. What is the rule of Christ?

NOTES

Introduction

1. Geddes MacGregor, *The Coming Reformation*, The Westminster Press, 1960, p. 17.

2. John White and Ken Blue, *Healing the Wounded: The Costly Love of Church Discipline*, InterVarsity Press, 1985, p. 23.

3. J. Carl Laney, *A Guide to Church Discipline*, Bethany House Publishers, 1985, p. 14.

Chapter 1

1. Quoted by Eduard Thurneysen, *A Theology of Pastoral Care*, John Knox Press, 1962, p. 47.

2. John Calvin, *Institutes of the Christian Religion*, Book 4, XI, 1.

3. Menno Simons, *The Complete Writings*, Herald Press, 1956, p. 989.

4. *Institutes*, Book 4, XI, 1.

5. Alfred Plummer, *An Exegetical Commentary on the Gospel According to St. Matthew*, Robert Scott, 1909, p. 229.

6. William Barclay, *The Gospel of Matthew*, vol. II, The Westminster Press, 1958, pp. 154-155.

7. Oscar Cullmann, *Peter: Disciple, Apostle, Martyr*, Meridian Books, Inc., 1958, pp. 184-212.

8. Wilhelm Vischer, *Die Evangelische Gemeindeordnung, Matthaus 16:13—20:18*, Evangelischer Verlag, 1946, p. 17.

9. Eduard Schweizer, *Church Order in the New Testament*, SCM Press, Ltd., 1961, p. 59.

10. Geddes MacGregor, *Corpus Christi*, The Westminster Press, 1958, pp. 103-104.

11. Barclay, pp. 206-207.

12. Ibid.

Chapter 2

1. Wayne Mack concurs. See Wayne Mack, *The Biblical Concept of Church Discipline*, Mack Publishing Company, 1974, chap. 6. The two chief dangers in church discipline, he says, are to be too harsh or to be too lenient.

2. Heinz Daniel Janzen, "Anabaptist Church Discipline in the Light of the New Testament," unpublished B.D. thesis, Biblical Seminary, New York, 1956, p. 26.

3. Menno Simons' classification, according to Frank C. Peters, "The Ban in the Writings and Life of Menno Simons," unpublished M.A. thesis, Toronto Graduate School of Theological Studies and Emmanuel College, 1953, p. 56. Menno's primary categories, however, are "falling" into sin and remaining in error. Persons in the former are to be repeatedly admonished, as necessary. Only those in the latter are to be excommunicated.

4. Robert White, "Oil and Vinegar: Calvin on Church Discipline," *Scottish Journal of Theology*, vol. 38, no. 1, 1985, p. 33.

5. Herbert Henley Henson, *Moral Discipline in the Christian Church*, Longmans, Green & Co., 1905, p. 60.

6. Nathaniel Marshall, *The Penitential Doctrine of the Primitive Church*, John Henry Parker, 1714, 1844, p. 197.

7. From Warwick Elwin, *Confession and Absolution in the Bible*, J. T. Hayes, 1883, p. 4. Pelliccia describes how the three classes of sins were matched by "three different kinds of punishment which the church used to inflict on offenders." See Alexis Aurelius Pelliccia, *The Polity of the Christian Church of Early, Medieval, and Modern Times*, J. Masters & Co., 1883, p. 417.

8. R. S. T. Haslehurst, *Some Account of the Penitential Discipline of the Early Church in the First Four Centuries*, SPCK, 1921, p. 32.

9. Quoted in Haslehurst, p. 36.

10. Walter A. Trobisch, "Congregational Responsibility for the Christian Individual," *Practical Anthropology*, Sept.-Oct., 1966, p. 199.

11. Max Thurian, *Confession*, SCM Press, Ltd., 1958, p. 43.

12. Rudolf Bohren, *Das Problem der Kirchenzucht im Neuen Testament*, Evangelischer Verlag, 1952, pp. 49-50.

13. Roger Ley shows what deplorable consequences followed from Zwingli's policing system initiated by the March 26, 1530, mandate. One of them was the loss of trust in pastors, who were forced into the role of prosecutors. *Kirchenzucht bei Zwingli*, Zwingli Verlag, 1948, p. 121.

14. The suggestion of the possibility of a fall from grace may not be palatable to Calvinists, who insist upon a rigid doctrine of the perseverance of the saints. If one does not allow the possibility of a fall from grace, the incidence of sin in the church and eventual excommunication for it must be construed as the exposure of a hypocrite, and that in turn will likely be explained in terms of an "invisible" church (i.e., promiscuous membership in the visible church).

We cannot go into a discussion of this issue here. It is enough to say that in the actual practice of discipline, the issue is not important. If an impenitent sinner is excluded from the church—whether as an exposed hypocrite or as one who falls from grace—the church's ground for this course of action remains the same. It must recognize that sinner's rejection of the grace proffered in the gospel.

15. Jay E. Adams, *Handbook of Church Discipline*, Ministry Resources Library, 1986, chap. 2.

16. Mark R. Littleton, "Church Discipline: A Remedy for What Ails the Body," *Christianity Today*, May 8, 1981, p. 31.

17. Adams, p. 35.
18. White and Blue, p. 99.

Chapter 3
1. Adams, p. 48.
2. Marshall, pp. 50-51.
3. Janzen, p. 66.
4. *The Complete Writings*, pp. 974ff.
5. Williston Walker, *The Creeds and Platforms of Congregationalism*, The Pilgrim Press, 1960, p. 228.
6. Littleton, p. 32.
7. James Leo Garrett, *Baptist Church Discipline*, Broadman Press, 1962, p. 42.
8. Heini Arnold, *The Plough*, Society of Brothers, June-July, 1987, p. 9.
9. In American Puritanism discipline was usually initiated by a charge filed against some individual for having broken the fourth, seventh, or tenth commandment. Emil Oberholzer, Jr., *Delinquent Saints*, Columbia University Press, 1956, passim.
10. Adams, pp. 30-31.
11. Such was the mistake of the elders in the publicized Oklahoma case of a few years ago. See Laney, chap. 11.
12. Adams' calls this a "contumacious" attitude, p. 72.
13. White and Blue, p. 22.
14. Adams, p. 61.
15. White and Blue, p. 124.
16. "The Tightrope: A Case Study in Church Discipline," *Leadership*, Summer, 1984.
17. Laney, p. 153, drawing also upon Daniel E. Wray, *Biblical Church Discipline*, The Banner of Truth Trust, 1978, p. 14.
18. This was another mistake of the church in the publicized Oklahoma case. The woman under discipline had hand-delivered a letter to the elders of the church requesting to withdraw her membership, but the church continued the disciplinary proceedings, nevertheless. Again, see Laney, chap. 11.
19. See the Feb. 7, 1986, issue of *Christianity Today* for the story of a doctor practicing abortions who asked to be dropped from membership in Moody Memorial Church, Chicago, when he came under its discipline. One member of the church executive committee, however, felt "the process of church discipline had been short-circuited," so he still attempted to confront the former member, apparently without success.
20. Laney, p. 159.

Chapter 4
1. Littleton, p. 33.
2. Adams, pp. 95-97.
3. Ibid., p. 54.
4. Don Baker, *Beyond Forgiveness: The Healing Touch of Church Discipline*, Multnomah Press, 1984.
5. Laney, p. 93.
6. The term used by White and Blue, p. 185.
7. For an account of the successful church discipline of a church leader that involved public confession, the interested reader might wish to look into Don Baker, *Beyond Forgiveness*.

Chapter 5

1. I would hesitate to accept Luther's statement that gamblers, revelers, drunkards, libertines, blasphemers, and mockers need not be banned, since they ban themselves by not going to Word and sacrament. (Luther adds that a pastor is to deny such persons all Christian ordinances from baptism to burial.) Ruth Götze, *Wie Luther Kirchenzucht Übte*, Vandenhoek & Ruprecht, 1958, pp. 14-15. Since there is not room for two levels of church membership—communing and communionless—the church must through admonition bring such people to faithful reception of communion or else endorse their rejection of grace by formal excommunication.

2. Pelliccia, pp. 484-485. Such a distinction was not known until the age of Gratian, says Pelliccia.

3. Article "Excommunication," *The Catholic Encyclopedia*, 1913.

4. See Elisabeth Vodola, *Excommunication in the Middle Ages*, University of California Press, 1986.

5. Edwin Lowell Adams, "A Study of Corrective Discipline in the Apostolic Church," unpublished doctoral dissertation, Southern Baptist Theological Seminary, Louisville, Kentucky, 1949, pp. 194-195.

6. Robertson and Plummer draw attention to Paul's use of *sarx* instead of *sōma* in 1 Corinthians 5:5. In Rom. 6:6, however, *sōma* is used. This inconsistency does not invalidate our point. If destruction of the "sinful body" does not denote physical suffering, "destruction of the flesh" is even less likely to, since *sarx* is the more characteristic Pauline expression for sinful human nature. See Archibald Robertson and Alfred Plummer, *First Epistle of St. Paul to the Corinthians*, Charles Scribner's Sons, 1916, p. 99.

7. Thurian, p. 46.

8. Thomas Witherow, *The Form of the Christian Temple*, T. & T. Clark, 1889, p. 153.

9. Williston Walker, p. 39.

10. Leon Morris, *The First Epistle of Paul to the Corinthians*, Wm. B. Eerdmans Publishing Company, 1958, p. 88. This view is also taken by the *Interpreter's Bible*.

11. Thurian, p. 46.

12. Article "Anathema" in *The Catholic Encyclopedia*.

13. Ibid.

14. *Institutes*, Book 4, XII, 10.

15. Haslehurst, p. 22.

16. Jean Lasserre, *War and the Gospel*, Herald Press, 1962, pp. 50-51.

17. Ley, p. 128.

18. E. Tyrrell Green, *The Church of Christ, Her Mission, Sacraments, and Discipline*, Methuen & Co., 1902, p. 339.

Chapter 6

1. Haslehurst, p. 26.

2. Williston Walker, p. 39.

3. Adams, pp. 71-75.

4. Ken and Joy Gage, p. 30.

5. Peters, p. 62, quoting Menno. On the practical application of his general rule Menno vacillated, and hesitated to go along with the "hard" banners. On the one hand he held that the ban was no respecter of persons, but on the other hand he said marital avoidance could not be forced upon people. He did write that shunning was in no way a temporary dissolution of the marriage. Ibid., pp. 97-99. In a Strassbourg meeting of 1557, fifty bishops from Alsace, Switzerland, Baden, Wurtemberg, and Moravia dis-

cussed shunning and rejected the severe position of Menno (as they understood it), and made clear that the command concerning marriage overrides that of the ban (meaning avoidance). Menno replied to the Strassbourg gesture in 1558 with "A Fundamental Doctrine . . ." in which "he expounded the ban in its strictest measures." Bauman reports that in early Dutch Mennonitism couples were interrogated at their wedding in the presence of the congregation as to their willingness to shun their spouse in case one should fall under the ban, and an affirmative answer was required. Irwin W. Bauman, "The Early Development of the Ban and Avoidance in the Mennonite Church," unpublished B.D. thesis, Harford Theological Seminary, 1926, p. 74.

6. David J. Markey, "An Inquiry into the Life and Teaching of Alexander Mack with Special Reference to His View of Church Discipline," unpublished M.A. thesis, 1954, pp. 94-95.

7. Marshall, Appendix I.

8. Ibid.

9. Haslehurst, p. 117.

10. Elwin, pp. 316-317. Beecher confirms this; he notes that a catechumen could not do penance because he was not a member of the church. Lyman Beecher, *The Antiquities of the Christian Church*, Gould, Newman and Saxton, 1841, p. 331. Marshall notes the discrimination: "When the party excommunicated was softened into submission, he was longer in recovering the privileges he had forfeited, than he was at first in gaining them; nor could he be readmitted to communion upon terms so easy as those upon which he was first admitted to it. And therefore, the penitent passed through more stages, and was longer detained from communion, than the catechumen." Marshall, pp. 49-50.

11. Oscar D. Watkins, *A History of Penance*, Longmans, Green & Co., 1920, vol. I, p. 482.

Chapter 7

1. Letter of Lois Barrett.

2. Mack, p. 6.

3. White and Blue, p. 19.

4. Heideman, "Church and Christian Discipline," *Reformed Review*, March, 1963, p. 29.

5. Warham Walker, *Church Discipline*, Gould, Kendall & Lincoln, 1844, p. 24.

6. Roy E. Knuteson, *Calling the Church to Discipline*, Action Press, 1977, p. 73.

7. Ibid., p. 132.

8. Ibid.

9. Lehman Hotchkiss in *Leadership*, Summer, 1984, p. 48. Emphasis by Hotchkiss.

10. Laney, p. 91.

Chapter 8

1. Alan Richardson, article "Devote" in *A Theological Word Book of the Bible*, The Macmillan Company, 1956, p. 68.

2. For further information on Jewish discipline see relevant articles such as those under "Ban" and "Excommunication" in *The Jewish Encyclopedia*, 1903, and *The Universal Jewish Encyclopedia*, 1941, and *Encyclopedia Judaica*, 1971.

3. R. H. Charles, ed., *The Apocrypha and Pseudepigrapha*, vol. II: *Pseudepigrapha*, At the Claredon Press, 1913, pp. 341-342.

4. S. L. Greenslade, *Shepherding the Flock*, SCM Press, Ltd., 1967, p. 92.

5. Bohren, p. 13.

6. According to Watkins, vol. 1, p. 472.

7. Marshall, pp. 50-51. Brackets Marshall's.

8. Haslehurst, p. 87.

9. Watkins, vol. I, p. 472.

10. Marshall, p. 53. Brackets Marshall's.

11. Ibid., p. 180.

12. Philip Schaff, *History of the Christian Church*, vol. II, Wm. B. Eerdmans Publishing Company, 1950, p. 189.

13. Watkins, vol. II, p. 755.

14. Watkins, vol. II, pp. 755-756. See also Henry Charles Lea, *A History of Auricular Confession and Indulgences in the Latin Church*, Lea Brothers & Co., 1896, and an introduction to the medieval penitentials in John T. McNeill and Helena M. Gamer, *Medieval Handbooks of Penance*, Columbia University Press, 1938.

15. Watkins, vol. II, p. 755.

16. Ibid., vol. II, p. 759.

17. Ibid., vol. II, p. 768.

18. Pelliccia, p. 442.

19. Lea, vol. I, pp. 36-37.

20. Vodola, *Excommunication in the Middle Ages*.

21. Ley, p. 6.

22. Wilhelm Maurer, *Gemeindezucht, Gemeindeamt, Konfirmation*, Im Johannes Stauda-Verlag zu Kassel, 1940, p. 9.

23. Götze, pp. 128-129.

24. Calvin also writes about Catholic abuses of excommunication: "Provided the domination of the clergy remains intact, provided no deduction is made from their tribute or plunder, almost anything is done with impunity, or carelessly overlooked.... True, they possess, under the name of excommunication, a tyrannical thunderbolt which they hurl at those whom they call contumacious. But what contumacy do they punish, unless it be of persons who, when cited to their tribunal about money matters, have either not appeared or, from poverty, have failed to satisfy their demands? Accordingly, the most salutary remedy for chastising the guilty, they merely abuse in vexing the poor and innocent." From *The Necessity of Reforming the Church* (1544), quoted in Robert White.

25. Article "Kirchenzucht" in *Realencyclopädie für protestantische Theologie und Kirche*, vol. X, 1901.

26. Luther continued to believe in and practice private confession, and the Augsburg Confession seeks to retain it. Frank C. Senn, "Structure of Penance and the Ministry of Reconciliation," *Lutheran Quarterly*, August, 1973.

27. Noted by William Klassen, *The Forgiving Community*, The Westminster Press, 1966, p. 180.

28. *Lutheran Cyclopedia*, Concordia Publishing House, 1954, p. 666.

29. See article "Church Discipline" in *The New Schaff-Herzog Encyclopedia*, 1952.

30. Article "Kirchenzucht" in the 1912 edition of *Religion in Geschichte und Gegenwart*.

31. Says Robert White, p. 25.

32. Article "Kirchenzucht" in *Realencyclopädie*.

33. "Church Discipline" in *The New Schaff-Herzog Encyclopedia*.

34. Quoted from Thurneysen, pp. 32-33.

35. Article "Discipline" in Hastings, *Encyclopedia of Religion and Ethics*. Scholars interested in the subject of Reformed discipline should see, besides the Robert White

article already cited, J. Wayne Baker, "Church Discipline or Civil Punishment: On the Origins of the Reformed Schism, 1528-1531," *Andrews University Seminary Studies*, Spring, 1985, and Mark E. VanderSchaaf, "Archbishop Parker's Efforts Toward a Bucerian Discipline in the Church of England," *Sixteenth Century Journal*, April, 1977. Robert White says that "although the consistory records have thus far been only partially examined, studies suggest a high frequency of cases involving quarreling and related anti-social behaviour, a preference for reprimand rather than excommunication, and a notable impartiality as to sex or social rank. When excommunication was pronounced (on an average, over 200 times a year between 1557 and 1560), it was usually of brief duration, requiring the guilty party to miss one of the four annual Communions. While the consistory's concern for morals could at times be vexacious and intrusive, its reputation as an agent of terror does not appear to be deserved" (pp. 36, 37).

36. See the doctoral dissertations by Ervin Schlabach, "The Rule of Christ Among the Early Swiss Anabaptists," 1977, and Jean Runzo, "Communal Discipline in the Early Anabaptist Communities of Switzerland, South and Central Germany, Austria, and Moravia, 1525-1550," 1978. See bibliography for publisher information.

37. Edited by J. C. Wenger, *The Mennonite Quarterly Review*, July, 1945, pp. 244-253. See also Kenneth R. Davis, "No Discipline, No Church: An Anabaptist Contribution to the Reformed Tradition," *The Sixteenth Century Journal*, XIII, no. 4, 1982.

38. Ervin Schlabach, "The Rule of Christ Among the Early Swiss Anabaptists."

39. Menno Simons, *The Complete Writings*.

40. David J. Markey.

41. In Eugene F. Roop, "The Brethren and Church Discipline (I)," in *Brethren Life and Thought*, Spring, 1969, p. 92. Part II appeared in the Summer, 1969, issue.

42. Article "Church Discipline" in Hastings, *Encyclopedia of Religion and Ethics*.

43. According to Geddes MacGregor, *Corpus Christi*, p. 105.

44. A comprehensive account of church discipline among the New England Puritans is Emil Oberholzer, Jr., *Delinquent Saints*, a study of all church discipline cases up to about 1830 found in the available records of those Massachusetts Puritan churches founded before 1765.

45. James R. Lynch, "English Baptist Church Discipline to 1740," *Foundations*, April-June, 1975, p. 123.

46. Ibid.

47. Ibid.

48. See Frederick Norwood, *Church Membership in the Methodist Tradition*, The Methodist Publishing House, 1958.

49. Liston O. Mills, "The Relationship of Discipline to Pastoral Care in Frontier Churches, 1800-1850: A Preliminary Study," *Pastoral Psychology*, December, 1965, p. 34.

50. Ibid., p. 32.

51. Larry James, " 'In the world but not of the world': Church Discipline in Antebellum Mississippi and Louisiana Baptist Churches," *Restoration Quarterly*, vol. 25, no. 2, 1982, p. 95.

52. Ibid., pp. 95-97.

53. Ibid., pp. 83-84.

54. See article "Kirchenzucht" in *Religion in Geschichte und Gegenwart*, 1959.

55. Hans Dürr, "Kirchenzucht in den Missionskirchen—und bei uns?" in *Festschrift für D. Albert Schädelin*, Verlag Herbert Lang & Cie, 1950, pp. 156-162.

56. Lesslie Newbigin, *The Household of God*, Association Press, 1954, p. 7.

57. White and Blue, p. 72. The interested reader may look into John R. Davis,

"Cross-Cultural Discipline," and Walter A. Trobisch, "Congregational Responsibility for the Christian Individual," both in *Practical Anthropology*, Sept.-Oct., 1966.

Chapter 9

1. Emil Brunner, *The Divine Imperative*, The Westminster Press, 1947, pp. 558-559.
2. Gerhard Ebeling, *Kirchenzucht*, W. Kohlhammer Verlag, 1947, p. 10.
3. F. John Taylor, *The Church of God*, The Canterbury Press, 1946, p. 156.
4. White and Blue, p. 21.
5. Wray, p. 1.
6. Laney, p. 12, quoting Luis Palau.
7. Knuteson, p. 16. Not everyone shares the concern for the recovery of church discipline. "The decline in traditional discipline signifies a more proper approach to the church," writes one Lutheran pastor. "When all is said and done, the fact that discipline has declined is a blessing, and it ought to remain a peripheral concern." Joseph Burgess, "The Decline of Discipline," *Dialog*, Summer, 1973, p. 216.
8. Quoted in Laney, p. 38.
9. Such individualism is now being deplored even in secular circles. See Robert Bellah, et al., *Habits of the Heart: Individualism and Commitment in American Life*, University of California Press, 1985.
10. Haddon Robinson, quoted in Littleton, p. 31.
11. I do not find credible Eugene Heideman's statement that "since the beginnings of the American republic the arena which has been marked off as beyond the control of the state has consistently increased." "Discipline and Identity," *Reformed Review*, Fall, 1981, p. 19.
12. Lynn R. Buzzard and Lawrence Eck, *Tell It to the Church: Reconciling Out of Court*, David C. Cook, 1982.
13. J. Carl Laney, "Church discipline without a lawsuit," and Lynn R. Buzzard, "Is church discipline an invasion of privacy," *Christianity Today*, Nov. 9, 1984.
14. Adams, p. 86ff.
15. Don Baker, p. 29. "Today formal discipline is being replaced by counseling," says Eugene P. Heideman in "Discipline and Identity," *Reformed Review*, Fall, 1981, p. 17.
16. Adams, p. 11.
17. Chapter 12, "Church Discipline in America."
18. J. Howard Kauffman and Leland Harder, *Anabaptists Four Centuries Later*, Herald Press, 1975.
19. Williston Walker, pp. 143-148.
20. Knuteson, p. 133. A similar tale is told by Adams, pp. 107-108. The term "church hopper" is actually Adams's.
21. See also Laney, pp. 159-160. Adams suggests guidelines drawn up by the local ministerium, if possible, p. 107.
22. Adams, p. 103.

Chapter 10

1. Quoted in Archibald Hunter, *Interpreting the Parables*, The Westminster Press, 1960, p. 33.
2. Joachim Jeremias, *The Parables of Jesus*, Charles Scribner's Sons, 1955, p. 157.
3. Clarence Tucker Craig, for example, balances them against each other in *The One Church*, Abingdon Cokesbury Press, 1951, p. 37.
4. Bohren, p. 56.

5. Götze, p. 126.

6. Ley, p. 33.

7. William Palmer, *A Treatise on the Church of Christ*, J. G. F. & J. Rivington, 1842, vol. I, p. 228.

8. Jonathan Edwards, *Works*, Isaiah Thomas, Jr., 1808, vol. I, p. 289.

9. Hunter, pp. 45-46.

10. Jeremias, p. 155.

11. Hunter, pp. 45-46.

12. C. H. Dodd, *The Parables of the Kingdom*, Collins, 1961, pp. 138-139.

13. Ibid.

14. Jeremias, p. 155.

15. Dodd, pp. 140-141.

16. Bohren, pp. 56-58.   Bohren refers in this connection to Paul's remark in 1 Cor. 5:12, "For what have I to do with judging outsiders?"

17. Walter Hobhouse,   *The Church and the World in Idea and in History*, Macmillan and Co., Ltd., 1910, pp. 395-396.

18. Menno Simons, *The Complete Writings*, p. 605.

19. *Luther's Meditations on the Gospels*,   trans. and arranged by Roland H. Bainton, The Westminster Press, 1962, p. 74. The somewhat uncommon thought that one should hesitate to uproot the tares because they might become wheat (which Luther mentions first) is not really the point of the parable, but comes closer to the spirit of it than do many other interpretations.

20. Emil Brunner,   *Dogmatics*, vol. III: *The Christian Doctrine of the Church, Faith and the Consummation*, The Westminster Press, 1962, pp. 28-29.

21. Quoted in Norwood, p. 74.

Chapter 11

1. Witherow, p. 147.

2. Ferdinand Probst, *Kirchliche Disciplin in den drei ersten christlichen Jahrhunderten*, Verlag der H. Lauppschen Buchhandlung, 1873, p. 385.

3. Ebeling, pp. 53-55.

4. John Potter, *A Discourse of Church Government*, S. Potter & Co., 1824, p. 304.

5. Ebeling, p. 56.

6. J. R. Mantey, "The Mistranslation of the Perfect Tense in John 20:23, Matthew 16:19, and Matthew 18:18," *Journal of Biblical Literature*, vol, 58, 1939, pp. 243-249. Howard in the *Interpreter's Bible* also notes the periphrastic future perfect in this text, claiming it "implies insight into a granting or withholding of forgiveness already determined in the divine judgment," vol. VIII, p. 798.

7. Ibid.

8. Henry J. Cadbury, "The Meaning of John 20:23, Matthew 16:19, and Matthew 18:18," *Journal of Biblical Literature*, vol. 58, 1939, pp. 251-254.

9. Hans Freiherr von Campenhausen, *Kirshliches Amt und geistliche Vollmacht in den ersten drei Jahrhunderten*, J. C. B. Mohr [Paul Siebeck], 1953, p. 137.

10. Craig, p. 34.

11. Ibid., pp. 34, 42.

12. Campenhausen, p. 153.

13. Newbigin, p. 55.

14. William Stewart, *The Nature and Calling of the Church*,   The Christian Literature Society, 1958, p. 77.

15. Thurian, pp. 51-52.   We would prefer the term *mediates* to the term *entails.*

BIBLIOGRAPHY

Books of General Interest

Adams, Jay E. *Handbook of Church Discipline*. Grand Rapids: Zondervan, 1986. Conservative and orthodox Presbyterian offers systematic and even dogmatic advice, but covers a lot of topics in commendable detail.

Baker, Don. *Beyond Forgiveness: The Healing Touch of Church Discipline*. Portland: Multnomah Press, 1984. The story of one successful case of the discipline of a pastor.

Buzzard, Lynn, and Eck, Lawrence. *Tell It to the Church*, Elgin, Ill.: David C. Cook Publishing Co., 1982. Not strictly about church discipline as here discussed, but an eloquent plea for reconciliation in the church rather than civil litigation.

Concern No. 14. A Pamphlet Series for Questions of Christian Renewal (Scottdale: Concern, 1967). Lead item is a John Howard Yoder exegesis of "Binding and Loosing" in Matt. 18:15-20.

Garrett, James Leo. *Baptist Church Discipline*. Nashville: Broadman Press, 1962. Introduction to and reprint of an early American Baptist discipline.

Greenslade, S. L. *Shepherding the Flock*. London: SCM Press, Ltd., 1967. A missionary reviewing early church discipline and suggesting possible applications in today's younger churches.

Knuteson, Roy E. *Calling the Church to Discipline.* Nashville: Action Press, 1977. A pastor's "Scriptural Guide" calls today's church back to the conscientious exercise of discipline.

Laney, J. Carl. *A Guide to Church Discipline.* Minneapolis: Bethany House Publishers, 1985. One of the better recent theologies of church discipline. By a Conservative Baptist seminary professor.

Mack, Wayne. "The Biblical Concept of Church Discipline." Cherry Hill, N.J.: Mack Publishing Company, 1974. A booklet with a somewhat Calvinist interpretation of church discipline.

Rowdon, H. H. "Puritan Church Discipline." Annual Public Lecture. London: London Bible College, [1960]. A pamphlet urging the recovery of church discipline in modern evangelicalism.

Shelly, Maynard (ed.). *Studies in Church Discipline.* Newton: Mennonite Publication Office, 1958. Essays on problems of discipline in the church. Tends toward the practical rather than the theological.

White, John, and Blue, Ken. *Healing the Wounded: The Costly Love of Church Discipline.* Downers Grove: InterVarsity Press, 1985. A counselor and pastor offer a summons and illustration-filled guide to church discipline.

Wray, Daniel E. "Biblical Church Discipline." Carlisle, Pa.: The Banner of Truth Trust, 1978. A booklet on the purpose and method of discipline, including a dozen answers to objections.

Books for Scholars

Bohren, Rudolf. *Das Problem der Kirchenzucht im neuen Testament.* Zollikon-Zürich: Evangelischer Verlag, 1952. Good theological analysis but very Calvinist view on the perseverance of the saints.

Götze, Ruth. *Wie Luther Kirchenzucht Übte.* Göttingen: Vandenhoeck & Ruprecht, 1958. A review of Luther's record that faces up to his mistakes but cannot question the source of those mistakes in his two-kingdom theology.

Haslehurst, R. S. T. *Some Account of the Penitential Discipline of the Early Church in the First Four Centuries.* London: SPCK, 1921. Good survey.

Jeschke, Marlin. *Toward an Evangelical Conception of Corrective*

Church Discipline. Doctoral Dissertation to Northwestern University, 1965. Obtainable from University Microfilms, 300 North Zeeb Road, Ann Arbor, MI 48106. The present author's first exploration into this subject, which, though dated, contains some references to the literature in the field and technical discussions not included in the present work.

Lea, Henry Charles. *A History of Auricular Confession and Indulgences in the Latin Church.* 3 Vols. Philadelphia: Lea Brothers & Co., 1896. Good survey of this era of the church.

Ley, Roger. *Kirchenzucht bei Zwingli.* Zürich: Zwingli Verlag, 1948. Criticism and defense of this Reformer's discipline theory and practice.

Marshall, Nathaniel. *The Penitential Doctrine of the Primitive Church.* Oxford: John Henry Parker, 1844 reprint of 1714 edition. An Anglican commends the early church for its firm discipline and advocates bringing some of it into the Anglican Church.

McNeill, John T., and Gamer, Helena M. *Medieval Handbooks of Penance.* New York: Columbia University Press, 1938. Fine scholarly study.

Menno Simons. *The Complete Writings.* Translated by Leonard Verduin. Edited by J. C. Wenger. Scottdale: Herald Press, 1956. Contains three essays on Menno's position on church discipline. In the second and third a beleaguered Menno is in polemic with the "hard banners."

Oberholzer, Emil, Jr. *Delinquent Saints.* New York: Columbia University Press, 1956. A review of discipline in New England Puritanism, which is not too sympathetic because it tends to follow the stereotype of Puritanism.

Vodola, Elisabeth. *Excommunication in the Middle Ages.* Berkeley: University of California Press, 1986. Well-researched study, useful for those prepared to learn the vocabulary of medieval secular and canon law.

Walker, Warham. *Church Discipline.* Boston: Gould, Kendall & Lincoln, 1844. A remarkably perceptive and comprehensive theological statement of the doctrine of church discipline.

Watkins, Oscar D. *A History of Penance.* 2 vols. London: Longmans, Green & Co., 1920. Thorough survey of the subject indicated.

SCRIPTURE INDEX

GENERAL INDEX

THE AUTHOR

Marlin Jeschke is professor of philosophy and religion at Goshen College in Goshen, Indiana, where he has taught since 1961. He received his B.A. from Tabor College and his degrees in theology from Garrett Theological Seminary (now Garrett Evangelical) and Northwestern University in Evanston, Illinois.

In 1968-69 he received a fellowship in Asian Religions for study at the Center for World Religions at Harvard University Divinity School. The fellowship included travel in Muslim and Buddhist countries of the Middle East, Southeast Asia, and Japan. In 1976 he participated in a National Endowment for the Humanites summer seminar on contemporary Marxism. In 1988-89 he was on sabbatical at Fuller Theological Seminary in Pasadena, California.

Jeschke has engaged in considerable research on the relationship of Christianity and Judaism, on a Christian approach to criminal justice, on modern religious movements, on Christology, and on eschatology. These studies indicate his interest in making the Christian faith relevant for today's world.

Professor Jeschke is book review editor of *The Mennonite Quarterly Review* and is the author of *Believers Baptism for Children of the Church* (Herald Press, 1983). He and his wife are members of College Mennonite Church and make their home in Goshen, Indiana.

262.9
J58

withdraw
1st ed

"Discipling the
    Brother"